PENGUIN HANDBOOKS

## *Gymnastics for Girls*

Dr. Frank Ryan, who holds a Ph.D.
in psychology, was for many years
the varsity coach at Yale University
in New Haven and is renowned for his
success in applying his techniques
for the physical and mental condi-
tioning of athletes in all sports.

DR. FRANK RYAN

# Gymnastics for Girls

PENGUIN BOOKS

Penguin Books Ltd, Harmondsworth,
Middlesex, England
Penguin Books, 625 Madison Avenue,
New York, New York 10022, U.S.A.
Penguin Books Australia Ltd, Ringwood,
Victoria, Australia
Penguin Books Canada Limited , 2801 John Street,
Markham, Ontario, Canada L3R 1B4
Penguin Books ( N.Z.) Ltd, 182–190 Wairau Road,
Auckland 10, New Zealand

First published in the United States of America
in The Viking Library of Sports Skills
by The Viking Press 1976
Published in Penguin Books 1977
Reprinted 1977, 1978

Copyright © Frank Ryan, 1976
All rights reserved

LIBRARY OF CONGRESS CATALOGING IN PUBLICATION DATA
Ryan, Frank.
Gymnastics for girls.
(A Penguin handbook)
Reprint of the ed. published by The Viking Press, New
York, in series: The Viking library of sports skills.
1. Gymnastics for women.    I. Title.
[GV464.R9 1977]      796.4′1      77-5307
ISBN  0 14 046.271 6

Printed in the United States of America by
The Book Press, Brattleboro, Vermont
Set in Linotype Caledonia

# Contents

# Introduction

All of us should have the great benefits that sports participation has to offer. The trouble has been that for ages only boys were encouraged to participate. Sports activity for girls was frowned upon and, in fact, often prohibited by law. But our society has finally seen the light. Girls can now participate in nearly every athletic activity, and they are doing so in increasing numbers.

If, for example, a girl wants to run, jump, or throw she now has the opportunity. She can turn to almost any sport that she enjoys. But girls' gymnastics is a very special case. The events are unique and especially designed for girls.

Because of their histories most sports have placed an enormous premium on strength—and they still do. The top shot-putters and discus throwers are extremely powerful men. Girls can enjoy these events and should if they wish, but they ought to realize that they are in events designed for males.

But during the last generation gymnastics for girls has broken away from imitating the activities of the men. Special events have been developed. No longer is there a premium on great physical strength. Instead, a show of strength is discouraged. Emphasis now is on graceful feminine activity. So the great appeal of girls' gymnastics results from its history—the deliberate and intelligent effort to modify it. For this reason gymnastics has become the most appropriate sport for girls.

There are four international gymnastics events for girls. We have floor exercise, balance beam, uneven parallel bars, and the vault. All four events have enormous attraction for the participants and the many millions of fans all over the world. We have had the exciting challenge of putting together this book on the four events; a book that we hope you will find useful.

The consultants throughout the entire effort have been Sandy and Jim Oldham. Highly qualified consultants have been the key to the entire Viking Library of Sports Skills series. We search for people as consultants who have original and clear views, who have enthusiasm, who have a record of highly successful teaching, and who enjoy the esteem of their colleagues. Sandy and Jim Oldham more than meet these qualifications. Through their dedicated teaching in many parts of the nation, they have personally influenced literally thousands of young people—and they are still doing so. Both have competed in gymnastics at high levels, and they have coached extensively. For many months they have met with me both for photo sessions and for long personal discussions. More than tolerant, they were always pleasant in responding to my questions. You will become acquainted with them via the photos throughout this book. I wish that I had words adequate enough to pay tribute to the amazing young ladies who appear in the pictures. They started early in the morning and stayed late. Weather made no difference. There was never even a hint of complaint. They were always cooperative and charming, and they showed a delightful and penetrating curiosity about the book. It was no surprise to learn that they are honor students and highly popular among their classmates. Perhaps these qualities are related to their participation in gymnastics.

About Bob Reid, our chief photographer, I hesitate to say much, for who would believe his extraordinary qualifications? He is an expert on all phases of communication—television, radio, motion pictures, educational theory, etc. His influence is seen in the photos, but it really extends far beyond that. He has been involved in the entire thinking and planning that went into this volume. Bob's attractive daughter, Nancy, was always on hand to lend assistance. This satisfaction of the talented and dedicated people who have worked together to bring you this book will depend upon your enjoyment of gymnastics.

## PLAN OF THIS BOOK

*Photos.* It is always difficult to describe action by words alone. Even the most carefully selected words are seldom adequate, for they can leave the reader with vague and sometimes inaccurate impressions. Photos can do a much better job of communication and so we have relied heavily on pictures to present our account. We cannot and do not avoid words entirely, but so far as possible words are closely tied to the pictures.

*Our guides.* The girls who demonstrate for us are all from the same junior high school, and all are pupils of Sandy Oldham. It is still very early in their careers, and they can't be expected to show perfect form in all their demonstrations. And that is all to the good for us. Like you, they are learning and progressing. You can identify with them as they illustrate the learning process.

*Progression.* In learning a sports event we start with the simpler skills and then gradually build toward mastery of the more complex skills. No progression can be completely foolproof. Sometimes girls will quickly learn a skill that experts consider difficult and then have some trouble with a simpler skill. Yet it is highly useful to arrange a progression of skills, a kind of ladder based both on expert opinion and logic. Hence, in this book one skill prepares the way for the next.

As you move up the ladder of skills, don't worry about the time element. You can't be on any ironclad schedule of progression; progression and its rate will surely vary from gymnast to gymnast. You and your coach should decide when you are ready for another step forward. Each stage in your learning is meant to be enjoyed. Even though you will be looking ahead to the mastery of increasingly advanced vaults, there is satisfaction and achievement to be found at each level. And when you get the chance to compete, enjoy it.

# Gymnastics for Girls

# *Floor Exercises*

## ABOUT FLOOR EXERCISE

What is floor exercise? Until fairly recently not many people knew. Long descriptions would have been needed to give a clear picture of the nature of floor exercise. But not any more. The world now knows. There has been a fantastic growth in its popularity. During the last Olympic Games this spectacular and dramatic sports event held hundreds of millions of television viewers spellbound. Excitement and interest now exists throughout the world. Spectators delight in gymnastics, but the great rewards go to the girls who actually participate.

In international and other formal competitions there are four official events. Floor exercise is one of them and probably the most attractive. Unlike the other three events, floor exercise does not involve apparatus. There are no beam, no uneven parallel bars, and no vaulting horse. There is just space. Space alone is the setting for the performance.

The space used in competition is a square area of 12 by 12 meters. That means that each side is a little less than 40 feet. The time allowed for a performance is between one minute and a minute and one-half. Floor exercise is carried out to music, and the music is important to performance. Only a single musical instrument can be used. It's usually a piano. The music is carefully selected to enhance the performance and to fit the personality of the performer.

*Scoring.* Even without any system of scoring, floor exercise would provide fun and satisfaction. But scoring allows competition and in this way increases the pleasure of the event. In gymnastics, scoring is different from the methods used in most other sports events. Judgment and the impression made are all-important in gymnastics. There can't, for example, be the precision that exists in track and field, where the results can be determined by the stopwatch and tape measure. And, of course, in other sports that we know so well scoring depends on the goal, the touchdown, or the basket. The judgment of the officials plays a part, but only to enforce rules.

Assigning victory without objective measurement has a long and rich tradition. When the ancient Greeks held their Olympic Games, it was beauty of performance that really mattered. Even the discus thrower, whose effort could have been measured with precision, was judged on the beauty of his performance.

In the ancient tradition, your floor-exercise routine will be judged by its beauty. And, of course, "Beauty lies in the eyes of the beholder." Beauty then is an impression. Our impressions of what is beautiful do differ somewhat, but we all share many impressions in common. For example, the great paintings please many millions in all parts of the earth. All of us enjoy a colorful sunset. So it is with floor exercise. Most of us can sense and enjoy a fine performance.

When a great floor-exercise performance takes place, nearly everyone in the audience knows it and thrills to it. In a way the judges represent the audience. Like the rest of the audience, they react to their general impressions. But they also have special training which makes their perceptions sharper.

For the precise scoring it's necessary to look at a rule book, a current one for the rules can change. For a high score certain "difficulties" have to be included in a routine. The rule book will tell you what the judges are looking for and how points are determined.

*Ingredients.* The goal of floor exercise is to present a fine composition. All of the elements or ingredients blend together for a fine performance. This is true in literature and music. But literature is made up of words and music of notes. Even a masterpiece of gourmet cooking is derived from an expert use of ingredients. So it is with floor exercise. You blend the ingredients to produce a pleasing result. Of course, that means that you have to know the ingredients.

The human being is capable of a great range of movements in space. The pleasing ones are those that interest us. They are the ingredients for floor exercise. Now, the body movements that we call ingredients can be and have been classified in various ways. Some experts group these movements in as many as five or even more categories. But a simpler approach would seem to be to just use two groupings—tumbling skills and dance skills.

*Variety of skills.* If one examines all other sports, it does look as if gymnastics requires more skills than any other sport. To learn these many skills takes great dedication, but then the satisfaction is very great. The gymnast is perhaps the most complete of all athletes. Though there does seem to be a bewildering number of skills to be learned, things are not as difficult as they appear. Learning one skill often helps you learn the next one.

*In what order should you learn the skills?* Well, it's difficult to know for sure. It does seem clear that some skills are simpler than others; and it does seem a good idea to progress from the simpler to those that are more difficult. In general, this book has paid attention to that notion. But the classification of skills from novice to expert is not always realistic. Some gymnasts may have trouble with a simple skill and then quickly master one that is considered advanced. Yet there has to be some order in which skills are learned. This book has tried to take account of that.

*Training and endurance.* The girl who does well in gymnastics is a well-conditioned athlete. In all sports the "record explosion" can be attributed to more and more work. The runners run and the swimmers swim mileage no one would have thought possible a few years ago. The top gymnast does not lag behind them. In fact, she puts in a more thorough day than the best professional football players. In training for floor exercise a good procedure is to work so that you can carry out your routine three times in a row.

## THE WARM-UP

Sometimes the beginner has to be reminded about the warm-up—but never the experienced athlete. The great performer is completely convinced that the warm-up is an essential part of the day's workout. There is no need for a reminder from the coach.

Though the warm-up has always been recognized as an important part of athletic preparation, the emphasis has become even greater over the years. The great athlete never did skip his warm-up, but today it is given more time and attention.

The basic purpose of the warm-up has always been to prepare the body for the work that is to come. The muscles are able to perform better. Blood moves to the muscles, and they are more pliable; a stretching of the muscles means that they can work better and with less chance of injury. But the basic idea of the warm-up has been extended—especially in gymnastics. The warm-up now develops greater flexibility and strength. Even skills are included. No matter what goals may be included, the warm-up starts with smooth and easy movements, and then there is a gradual increase in effort.

Any warm-up can be selected from a vast number of possible exercises. But the selection should be meaningful to the event. For example, the runner spends much of his warm-up in running. The baseball pitcher throws to warm up. So it is with the gymnast who uses gymnastic skills. The great realm of useful warm-up exercises is too large to include many of them. But we can show a few that are representative.

## General

**1.** Here the trunk, arms, and legs swing easily and smoothly. In *a* and *b*, side, or lateral body stretch. The full body is exercised. A straight back forward stretch (*c*), in which the legs are also stretched. In *d* the back is rounded, and the hamstrings (muscles in the back of the upper leg) are stretched. The rest of the photos show various full-body and stretching movements. A warm-up can be selected from a great variety of exercises.

1*a*

1*d*

1*e*

1b

1c

1f

1g

# Flexibility

**2.** Again, a few of a lot of possible exercises. In *a*, a sitting position with the feet together. The knees are kept down while the back remains straight. The muscles of the inner thigh are stretched. This exercise prepares for straddles and splits. At the same time, back strength is developed. In *b* the legs are kept straight while the head moves forward and down to the mat. In *c*, a straddle sitting position with a lateral flexion, the legs are stretched and there is a torso stretch. A stretch forward in *d*; the trunk is completely flat. In *e* and *f* the shoulder girdle and upper back are stretched. The position in *e* was reached from a lying position. Vision is on the fingers. Heels are flat and the arms straight. In *f* the legs are straightened to flex the shoulders even further.

These flexibility exercises do look difficult, and you can't really expect to carry them out perfectly right away. At first, you many have to do them partially, but with time and effort you will be able to carry them out fully.

2c

2d

2a

2b

2e

2f

## Strength

Though gymnastics for girls does not emphasize great strength, the gymnast is much stronger than the average girl. The skills do require more than ordinary strength. For this reason a part of the warm-up session is devoted to building the needed strength. As in all warm-ups, you can select from a great variety of exercises. The few that are included here are both typical and useful.

**3.** In *a* and *b*, sit-ups from a bent-knee position. The feet, tucked close to the seat, are held down by a partner. Photos *c*, *d*, *e*, *f*, and *g* show an important variation of the sit-up. It starts from a lying position (*c*) and goes to a V-seat with the hands forward of the legs (*e*). This exercise not only builds strength in the muscles of the stomach, it also develops timing and a skill that can be used in later performance. Photos *h* and *i* show a simple

push-up. The pushing strength developed by this exercise has become important to nearly all sports. Later on, you will see that the ability to push strongly with the arms is important to carrying out many skills. When starting, some girls are unable to make a full push-up, so a partial one must do. But a partial push-up still calls for full arm extension. It's just that you don't go all the way down to the mat.

3*c*

3*d*

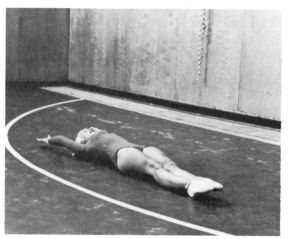

3*g*

3*h*

3a

3b

3e

3f

3i

# Forward Roll—Tuck Position

**4.** In *a* the tuck position is taken with the spotter ready to help. In *b* the hands have made contact with the mat. The hips are rising. The chin is moving toward the chest. Notice in *c* that the spotter is helping with the tuck of the head. The correct use of the arms is a key to a good roll. The arms bend to lower the head to the mat, but their bend is smooth and firm. Even by *c* the arms continue to support the main weight of the body. In this way the back of the head makes very gentle contact with the mat. The contact of the head is very brief, as the body weight passes almost immediately to the shoulders. The rounded body (*d*) and compact position help keep the body rolling. In *d* the arms have started to reach forward to help continue the roll and to give balance. By *e* the roll is completed and the position is like the starting one. The heels are close to the seat. Legs are tucked. The upper body is erect. Arms are stretched forward.

4a

4b

4c

4d

4e

# Forward Shoulder Roll to V Seat

**5.** The start (*a*) is being made from an extended stag position. Body weight is over one knee with the other leg extended. The arm movements (*a, b,* and *c*) add grace and make the start of the roll less abrupt. Photo *d* shows the right arm reaching back so that the hand is about even with the right foot. The high position of the hips is needed to give the head and shoulder room to get to correct position on the mat. By *e,* the shoulder has made contact with the mat. The right leg is still on the mat. The left leg is extended. As the roll continues, the legs come together and the arms are along the mat for balance (*f*). The roll finishes in a V seat (*g*) with the hands giving support.

The key photo in the series is *d,* where the hips are kept up and the reach of the arm is long.

5*a*

5*b*

5*e*

5c

5d

5f

5g

# Forward Roll to Straddle Lift Position

**6.** Starting (*a*) is in a straddle position. The back is flat and the arms are out to the side. In *b* the hands are on the mat, and the arms are bending to lower the upper body. The arms keep control so that the landing of the back of the head is very light. Taking the weight on the hands and tucking the head are both important. The roll is underway (*c*). In *d* the roll is almost completed. A straddle position is taken. Movement will continue until the upper body is well forward. In *e* the right hand reaches forward while the left hand reaches backward and is placed on the mat. Next (*f*), the right arm is swung upward as the hips are pushed up to a straddle lift position.

6a

6b

6c

6d

6e

6f

# Forward Roll to Straddle Stand Position

**7.** A straddle position and ready for the roll (*a*). In *b* we again see the two important keys to a good forward roll. Body weight is supported by the hands so that the head makes light contact with the mat, and the head is tucked so that its back touches the mat. The roll continues (*c*). Hand position (*d*) becomes important. The hands are flat on the mat and close to the body. Fingers are pointing forward. The shoulders are forward. This favorable position of the arms and shoulders permits a push into the straddle position (*e*). The legs are kept straight.

7*a*

7b

7c

7d

7e

# No-Handed Forward Roll

**8.** In the roll that we are watching, starting position is from a stand. This skill is somewhat more advanced than the previous rolls and calls for more flexibility. In *b* the body starts to lower and the head to tuck. The tucked head and the elevated hips (*c*) are key points. By *d* the back of the head has touched lightly and briefly, and the center of the roll has already moved to the shoulders. In *e*, with the roll almost completed, the right leg has bent to get ready to lift the body to a standing position. Back to the standing position (*f* and *g*).

The photos show the form that you will eventually want to have. But along the way you can practice on an easier basis. For example,

8a

8b

8e

while first learning you could start on your knees. Also, the hands can make light contact with the mat (about the point of photo *c*). But as your confidence grows, you will want to be able to carry out the roll as shown in the photos.

8c

8d

8f

8g

# Dive-Forward Roll

Here the dive-forward roll is being carried out from a standing position. It could also be carried out from a run with a two-foot jump take-off. The dive can emphasize either height or distance, but height seems far more pleasing.

**9.** As the dive starts (*c*), emphasis is on lift. It is useful to think of diving over a barrel. In *d* we can see that the hands are solidly placed, and the arms are easing the head to the mat. The legs are straight. The roll is completed in *e*, *f*, and *g*.

9*a*

9*d*

9*e*

9*b*

9*c*

9*f*

9*g*

# Egg Roll to Stag

The egg roll is one of the simpler skills, but it is a valuable one. In itself the egg roll is attractive, but it also places you in a good position to move to the next skill in the routine.

**10.** The start (*a*) is in a tuck position with the arms out to the side. In *b* one arm is brought inward and the roll started over the shoulder. The legs remain tucked (*c*). If you were only doing a simple egg roll, you could, by *e*, get back to the starting position of *a*. (But it's better to make the egg roll part of the larger picture of the routine.)

In *d* the left arm is straightened with the hand against the mat. By *e* the weight is over the bent left knee with the right leg extended. A stag kneeling position is reached (*f*). Arm movements add grace (*g* and *h*).

10*c*

10*f*

10*g*

10a

10b

10d

10e

10h

Later, we will be talking more about combinations, but if you go back a little in the book to the forward shoulder roll, you can see that it started from the position reached by the egg roll (h).

# Backward Roll, Tuck Position

**11.** The start is being made (*a*) from a tuck position. The arms are extended forward. You may hear the puzzling expression "You have to lean forward to roll backward." It means that the body weight should be forward to give you balance and control. Even in *b*, as the seat touches the mat, the arms are still reaching forward. The back is beginning to round. Of course, a rounded back is needed for a good rolling surface. The key to a rounded back is in head movement. When the head is tucked, the back tends to round.

In *c* the movement of the arms has started. By *d* the hands are firmly on the mat, with the fingers pointing toward the shoulders. Elbows are in. The goal is to position the arms so that

11*a*

11*b*

11*e*

11*f*

there can be a good pushing action. Spotting helps raise the hips (*d* and *e*). This lifting action by the spotter is especially important to beginners who may not have developed the needed strength.

In *e* you can see that the points of contact with the mat are the hands and the feet. Notice that the feet have changed their pointed position of *d* so that they can be gathered under the body. The change from the bent position of the arms (*e*) to a straight position (*f*) shows that a good push has been made. Back to the tuck position (*g*).

11*c*

11*d*

11*g*

# Back Shoulder Roll to Stag Sit Position

**12.** The start (*a*) is the same as seen in the backward roll (previous skill). But this time the roll is made over the shoulder. So in *c* we see the right arm moving to clear the way for the shoulder. Preparation to land on the right knee appears in *d*. The roll has been perfectly over the shoulder. The left leg remains extended.

Extension of the left leg is directly backward (*e*), and the left arm pushes (*e* and *f*) to lift the upper body. The push is partially backward so that there is sitting position on the heel. In *g* the arms are brought over the head to make for a graceful finish.

12*a*

12*d*

12*e*

12b

12c

12f

12g

# Back Roll—Straddle Position

**13.** The start is from a straddle position (*a*). With the start of the roll the arms reach well back so that the hands are placed beyond the feet (*b*). It's a good idea to watch the hands to make sure they are well back. As shown, the hands are placed between the legs. The fingers point forward. This position allows the arms to ease the body to the mat. From *c* to *d* the arms and hands move quickly so that they are positioned for the push. In *e* the push is underway. Back to straddle position (*f*).

13*a*

13*d*

13*b*

13*c*

13*e*

13*f*

# Back Roll—Pike Position

**14.** Another attractive variation of the backward roll. The skill starts from a standing position ($a$). In $b$ the upper body moves forward to the pike position. The roll starts, and in $c$ the arms have moved outside the legs and backward so that the hands can catch the weight of the body. The task is to move the hands quickly from their position in $d$ to that in $e$ so that you are ready to push. The push back to starting position appears in $f$, $g$, and $h$.

14a

14c

14f

14g

14b

14d

14e

14h

Throughout the roll the legs remain straight
with the feet together. You can see how
important arm action is. The arms move to
support the body and then to supply the push.

# Back Roll to Handstand—Walkout

**15.** From the standing position (*a*) the knees are bent to tuck (*b*). As in the other rolls the movement of the arms becomes key. They have to move quickly to the position shown in *c* so that they are ready for a push. From *c* to *d* the arms push upward, and the legs "shoot." Vision is on the hands. The entire body is stretched, with the toes pointed. Note the spotting. Here the spotting is at the knees, but if the performer is less experienced spotting is at the hips.

There are many ways that you can come out of the handstand. In this instance a simple walkout is used (*e*) with one leg dropping to the mat. The step is to a standing position (*g*).

15*a*

15*d*

15*e*

15b

15c

15f

15g

## Headstand in Tuck Position—Rollout

**16.** The start (*a*) is in a tuck position with the hands flat on the floor. Photo *b* is highly significant, because it shows a good base. The hands and the head form a triangle or tripod. The hands are placed far enough away from the head to make for a wide base. The head is in contact with the mat at about the hairline. It's important to establish a good base while the body is still low in the tuck position. Get balance early.

From *b* to *c* the legs are extended upward slowly and under control. There are various ways to come out of the headstand, but it's more pleasing not to come out in the same way you went into it. Here a forward roll is used. The chin is brought toward the chest, and the roll is on the back of the head, then on the shoulders (*d*). The legs are starting to tuck in *d*. The roll is continued (*e*) to the standing position (*f*).

16c

16d

## Handstand— Beginning Technique

**17.** When the start is made with the hands already in position (*a*) there is more confidence. The hands are flat on the floor about shoulder distance apart. Fingers point forward to give more support for the handstand and also to permit more power for any move out of the handstand. Spotting is at the hips (*b* and *c*). The body forms a straight line with the toes pointed (*c*).

17a

16a

16b

16e

16f

17b

17c

# Handstand—Kickup Technique

**18.** The previous technique, in which the start was made with the hands already in place on the mat, was shown because it's a good way to gain early confidence. Here, the starting position is from a stand (*a*). The arm action (*b*) makes the approach to the handstand more pleasing. In *c* the arms and the back leg almost form a straight line. The arms and upper body do not simply lower by themselves. Instead, as the arms lower, the free leg rises (*d*). In this way there is a graceful pivot about the center of the body. The hands (*e*) are placed about shoulder width with the fingers pointing forward. Spotting (*f*) is at the legs, though with beginners the spotting is often best done at the hips. The legs come together (*g*) to complete the handstand with the body in a straight line.

18*a*

18*b*

18*e*

18c

18d

18f

18g

## Some Handstand Positions

**19.** The various handstand positions are not held. Rather, they are moved through. In *a*, the split position. A double bent-leg position (*b*). This handstand is not only attractive but more easily controlled, because the leg position tends to balance the body. It also lends itself well to a further move such as a walkover. The yogi handstand (*c*) is somewhat more difficult to do, though it is attractive enough to justify the extra effort. The elbows have to be straight and locked. The head looks to the knees instead of the fingers. In the photo the legs are tucked, but they can also be straight.

19*a*

19b

19c

# Handstand to Forward Roll

**20.** The first four photos (*a*, *b*, *c*, and *d*) review the handstand kickup technique. In *c* we see that the free leg is high and extended as the hands make contact with the mat. Hands are shoulder-width, with the fingers forward. The handstand is completed in *d*. From *d* the arms lower the body to a headstand. It's important that the arms control the body weight and that the head be lowered easily to the mat. In *e* the head has tucked, and a headstand is achieved. The legs are still straight. The legs don't bend until the roll has moved to the back. The legs continue to bend until the heels are close to the seat (*g*). Up to the stand (*h*).

20*a*

20*b*

20*e*

20*f*

20c

20d

20g

20h

# Handstand from the Knees

**21.** An attractive way to reach a handstand. In *a*, a sitting position on the heels. By *b* momentum has been developed. The hands are placed on the mat close to the knees so that the straightening of the legs makes for a more effective push. In *c* the legs have completed their push, and the hips are rising. The legs are tucked in *d* and again extended in *e* to complete the handstand.

21*a*

21*d*

21b

21c

21e

# Cartwheel

In doing the cartwheel it's important to think of it as a sideways rather than a forward movement. It is helpful to think of yourself as a wheel with the arms and legs as the spokes.

**22.** Our performer is going to cartwheel to her right, so in the starting position (*a*) body weight is over the left leg with the right foot pointing to the side. In *b*, a reach sideways of the right arm. Weight has now shifted to the right leg with the left leg starting to kick up. You can see in *c* that the right hand is firmly planted, while the left is just making contact with the mat. The intervals between the "spokes" are important. The legs are starting to come up (*c*). In *d* the legs are straight and well apart. This makes for the "amplitude" which affects judging.

Most beginners have trouble getting their hips high and in line with the body. The spotter can help raise the hips (*c* and *d*). In this way

22a

22b

22e

22f

the beginner gets a feel for the correct hip position, and learning follows more easily.

In *e* the left leg nears the mat. As the foot touches, the arms are picked up right away so that the cartwheel can be continued to a standing position (*g* and *h*).

The wheel idea is important. One spoke at a time. It helps to work with a rhythmic count of one-two-three-four. Once the cartwheel is learned on the favorite side, it should be learned from the other side.

22c

22d

22g

22h

# One-Handed Cartwheel

**23.** The start is similar to that of the regular cartwheel (*a*, *b*, and *c*). Movement is to the side. Photo *d* shows good form, with the arm straight and both legs extended and apart. (If the beginner feels uneasy at this point, she can bring her other hand to the mat for support. But, of course, as soon as possible she gets back to using only one hand.) In *e* the lead leg continues so that it lands well in close to the hand. The cartwheel finishes in a stand (*f*, *g*, and *h*). In *h* the arms are raised. In this way the wheel image is kept from start to finish.

23a

23d

23e

23b

23c

23f

23g

23h

Though our subject moves to her right, she can
also use her left arm for the cartwheel. The
judges would regard this as a higher level of
difficulty.

# Cartwheel to a Split

**24.** There are many variations of this skill. In this photo sequence the cartwheel goes directly to a split. (You can go first to your feet and then split.) In *a* and *b* there is the start of a regular cartwheel. The spotter is in position to help raise the hips. When the inverted position is reached (*c*), the weight is shifted to the left hand. The right hand is cleared (*d*) to make room for the left leg to come through and split in *e*. If the split is carried out well, the left hand will be near the seat. Completion of the split is shown in *f*.

*24a*

*24d*

*24e*

24b

24c

24f

# Dive Cartwheel

**25.** The standing position (*a*) and the start of the run (*b*). Preparation for the hop or skip from the left leg (*c*). A European hurdle (*d*) in which the legs are held together. Landing from the hop is on the left foot (*e*) as the right foot moves forward. A firm push of the right leg lifts the body so that it is airborne. You can see in *f* that the hand is just making contact with the mat. The cartwheel is completed in *g* and *h*.

25a

25b

25e

25f

25c

25d

25g

25h

## Aerial Cartwheel

**26.** The approach is similar to that used in the dive cartwheel. The run (*b*) and readiness for the hop or skip (*c*). The European hurdle (*d*). The timing of the spotter is important. She prepares to spot at the hips (*c*, *d*, and *e*) and then carries out the job of helping with additional height. It takes experience to be a good spotter. When first learning to spot it's a good idea to have the subject perform with only one step. In this way timing can be learned.

In *f* body weight is over a somewhat flexed right leg—almost in the manner of a good highjumper. The leg extends (*g*), and the goal is to drive the hips high. The other leg whips to give both speed and height. The extended arms add beauty. The legs remain straight, and in *h* the toe is turned ready for the landing. Eyes are on the left foot so that it can be put down right under the nose. The recovery (*i*) and a good standing position (*j*).

26c

26d

26g

26h

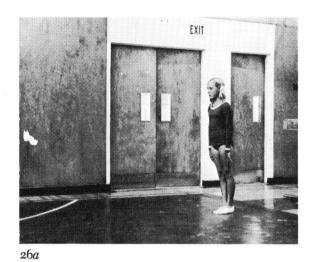

26a

26b

26e

26f

26i

26j

# Roundoff

**27.** The run (*a*, *b*, and *c*) is similar to that of the dive cartwheel. So are the first movements toward the mat (*d* and *e*). However, at the top of the cartwheel the legs are brought together. There is an instant handstand. The feet are brought together quickly, and the handstand is help for only a brief fraction of a second. There is a quarter-turn. The legs are snapped down in the direction from which the run started (*f*). At the same time that the legs are snapped down, the arms push. Notice in *f* that she is completely airborne. After the landing there is a rebound (*g*). The landing is in a straight up and down position.

27a

27d

27g

27h

27b

27c

27e

27f

Just to illustrate the roundoff a standing finish
is shown in *h*. But in a routine another stunt
would follow. The roundoff is a good way to
develop speed and, at the same time, change
the direction in which the body is facing.

## Headspring to a Tuck Position

**28.** The start is from a tuck position (*a*). The hand position (*b*) is different from that of the regular headstand, because the headstand position is passed through rather than held. So the tripod position of head and hands isn't needed. Instead, the hands are placed in line with the head so that there will be more power in the arms. The legs (*b* and *c*) are straight.

Their whip contributes to momentum, but timing is important. Both the whip of the legs and the drive of the arms start only after the hips have passed by the head.

Spotting (*c* and *d*) is on both the back and the arm. Lift is given to the back. The arm is helped to whip forward. Back to the tuck position (*e*).

28*a*

28b

28c

28d

28e

# Headspring to Stand

**29.** A start from the standing position (*a*). In *b* the knees are bending, and the upper body is starting toward the mat. By *c* the hands are placed on the mat in line with the head. Fingers are pointing forward. In *d* the head is on the mat, and the hips have gone past the vertical. The legs are whipping, and the arms are ready to push. The hips are kept high (*e*) and pushed forward. The legs extend to lift the body to a standing position (*f*).

Critical points are to make a hard forward drive of the hips and a strong push of the arms off the mat.

29*a*

29*d*

29*e*

29*b*

29*c*

29*f*

# Headspring to Pike

**30.** The now familiar start from a stand to a headspring (*a*, *b*, and *c*). Hands are placed in line with the head (*c*). Legs are extended and start their whip only after the hips have passed the vertical (*d*). The whip has to be strong, the body has to be extended and the arm push powerful. Landing is actually on the heels (*e*). You can see that the seat is still clear of the mat as the heels touch. The arms, after pushing, continue to whip forward. The arms reach forward to touch the toes (*f*).

30*a*

30*b*

30*d*

30*e*

30c

30f

This stunt can also be carried out to a straddle. The straddle should start very late so as not to interfere with the leg whip.

## Kip or Neck Spring

**31.** An attractive skill in floor exercise. But also kipping actions are important for other events such as the uneven parallel bars. The kip can be taken from a number of moves. In our sequence the kip is from a backward roll.

In *a*, the tuck position. The backward roll starts (*b*). In *c* the legs begin to straighten as she cradles back to the position seen in *d*. The *d* position is important. The hands have moved to a power position close to the head. The legs are nearly parallel to the mat. From this position the legs circle around and forward. They develop speed, and there is an effort to drive the hips forward. After the hips pass the vertical position (*e*), the arms begin their vigorous push. When the body lands (*f*) there is a back arch. Movement is continued to a straight position (*g*).

Spotting starts in *d*—a hand under the hips in case there is not enough whip. The spotter's right hand is near the legs to prevent a leg whip that might be too soon and too straight up.

31*a*

31*d*

31*e*

31b

31c

31f

31g

# Handspring to Stand

**32.** The running start (*a*) and hurdle (*b*). In *c*, a bend of the forward leg, and the hands go to the mat. Close to the handstand position (*d*). As she progresses further, our subject will have her legs close together at this point. Important to the position in *d* is to get the hands down quickly. The hands have to be on the mat before the legs pass the vertical. You can see that in *d* the hands have almost completed their push-off action. The push is from the hands and shoulders. The push is strong so that there will be time for the body to get around. By *e*, because of the height afforded by the push and the circular movement, landing is on the feet. The standing position (*f*).

The handspring to a stand is not entirely easy. In some cases it may be best if the landing is made to a squat position. Then you can advance to landing in a standing position.

The spotter in *c* is ready to get the closer arm and the hips or back. In the inverted position (*d*) spotting is on the back and the upper arm. In this way the spotter can offer both lift and help with the arm action.

32*a*

32*b*

32c

32d

32e

32f

## Handspring to Walkout

**33.** From the hurdle position, the right leg steps out (*a*). The hands come quickly to the mat (*b*) with the fingers pointing forward. Vision is toward the hands. The free leg starts upward. The legs stay apart. There is a strong push from the hands. Landing in *c* is on one foot. The free leg and the hips are thrust forward, and the movement continues to a standing position (*d*).

Though the legs are apart or in a stride position throughout, the technique of the handspring remains the same . . . hands quickly to the mat and a good push-off. The pushing forward of the free leg and hips are key points. The forward action of the hips is helped by allowing the head to remain back.

33*a*

33*d*

## Handspring to Straddle Sit

A very attractive exercise that should be used more often. The basic ideas of the handspring apply, but the timing is a bit different. The movement has to be slower to allow the legs to come close together.

**34.** The familiar run and hurdle (*a*). In *b* the hands drop to position. The slower timing is shown in *c*, allowing the legs to come together. The landing *d* is made in the straddle position with the heels touching first. The legs are straight. The forward position of the upper body is important in reaching the final position (*e*).

34*c*

33b

33c

34a

34b

34d

34e

# Front Limber

This skill is not used by itself too much, but its mastery is essential to other skills. To provide a good base the limber must be carried out smoothly and under control.

**35.** In *a*, readiness to kick to a handstand. Movement toward the handstand (*b* and *c*). In *d* the handstand is reached. Spotting insures a good handstand and helps with the feeling of control. The legs start to drop smoothly and under control (*e*). The line of vision is still on the hands, which helps set a good head position. In *f* the feet have dropped smoothly to the mat with the hands still in contact with the mat. This is a bridge position (you'll remember seeing it in the warm-up exercises). Some key points are seen. The hands and feet are not far apart. The toes are pointed forward. There is no attempt to get high up on the toes. There is no push with the hands until the feet have

35*b*

35*c*

35*f*

35*g*

touched. Just as the feet do touch the hand push is started to make for smoothness and continuity.

In *g* the forward thrust of the hips brings them forward of the feet. At this point, the arms and head remain back. The arms are never dropped. They remain in the position shown so that they can help in bringing the body to an erect position (*h*). The arms are upward.

35*a*

35*d*

35*e*

35*h*

The limber is different from the regular handspring in that it resembles a walking motion. The body is never completely airborne but always in contact with the mat.

## Arabian Limber

**36.** This skill is a variation of the front limber and a little bit more difficult to do. There is no jump at the start. Both feet are together (*a*). Both knees bend (*b*) and the hands are being brought to the mat. In *c* the hands are in correct position on the mat and the legs are pushing off. The hips are driven over the hands (*d*). Good abdominal strength is needed to pull the legs up to the handstand in *e*. From *e* various options exist, such as a walkout, but here the action is continued to a limber (*f*, *g*, and *h*).

36a

36b

36e

36f

36c

36d

36g

36h

# Forward Walkover

**37.** The limber has to be mastered before there can be a good walkover. In *a* and *b*, a step kickup to a handstand. The legs in *c* are in a stride position. Try for as full a split as possible. In *d* the lead leg has come down to the mat. As soon as the foot touches, the hips are driven forward and the arms brought upward. The extended right leg is thrust both forward and upward. The spotter's right hand helps keep the lead leg high, while the left hand helps with the forward motion. You can see that the spotter has to be on the correct side. In *e* the lead leg is straight ahead with the toes pointed. Arms are overhead. The finish (*f*), with the weight over the left leg, the right toe pointed, and arms upward.

A front walkover can also be carried out one-handed.

37*c*

37*d*

# Forward Walkover—Switch

**38.** The start and finish are similar to that of the regular walkover. The difference is the switch of the legs that takes place during the handstand. A stride position in *a*. By *c* positions of the legs are reversed, and a stride position is reached again. To carry out the switch the handstand has to be held somewhat longer than in the regular walkover. During learning the spotter helps hold the handstand position.

38*a*

37a

37b

37e

37f

38b

38c

# Forward Walkover to Knee (with a Half Turn to Split)

**39.** In *a*, readiness to kick up to a handstand position. The lead leg is bending in *b* and in *c* dropping toward the mat. The head is held high to help make for a good arch of the back. The bent leg does not come straight down. Instead, the leg continues to bend, and the heel is pulled backward. Contact with the mat is made by the instep or front part of the foot (*d*). The head is back and the arms have started their forward and upward movement.

(From this position you could go directly to a split.) Movement is to an upright position (*e*) with the right leg extended. In *f* the left leg is straightened, and a quarter turn is made. Another quarter turn (*g*) and to the split (*h*).

The spotting is like that for a regular walkover. Spotting is especially helpful (*c*) to give the bent lead leg a chance to get down smoothly and well back.

39*a*

39*b*

39*e*

39*f*

39c

39d

39g

39h

## Stag Fall to Front Walkover

**40.** Another attractive version of the walkover. In the starting position (*a*) body weight is one leg with the lead leg bent so that the foot touches the knee. Arms are overhead. The forward fall starts in *b*. The hips are pushed forward. The top of the foot is in contact with the mat. By *c* the roll is to the knee, and the hands have landed. The other leg is extending. As soon as the hands touch, the right leg begins to push to move the body to *d*, split-stride walkover position. The walkover is completed in *e*, *f*, and *g*.

*40a*

*40b*

*40e*

40c

40d

40f

40g

# Forward-Dive Walkover

**41.** This skill is somewhat similar to the dive cartwheel. There is an attempt to get early height. Unlike the handspring, height is gotten before the hands reach the mat. In *a*, the hurdle. The right leg (*b*) is coming forward to provide a strong take-off push for the needed height. In *c* the hands have not yet reached the mat. You can see that she has been completely airborne. By *d* the walkover is underway. The left foot is on the mat, and the hands have pushed. Arms come up (*e* and *f*) to finish the walkover. In *e* the head is still back and between the arms. Hips are forward.

41*a*

41*d*

41b

41c

41e

41f

# Mounding Front Walkover

**42.** The hurdle (*a*). A two-footed take-off with an effort to get good height. Photo *d* shows the tuck and good height. In *e* the hands are nearing the mat, and the legs are ready to go to stride position. Out of the walkover (*g*).

42*a*

42*d*

42*e*

42b

42c

42f

42g

## Backbend Kickover

**43.** The starting position (*a*) is straight up and down with the hands above the head. The first part of the body to move is the head (*b*). The hips come forward. The arms are moving toward the mat with the eyes looking at the fingers. The head is placed back—never thrown. Control is important. Too, the hands are placed smoothly on the mat. In *c* the kickover has started. The left leg is pushing, and the right leg is kicking. The push and kick bring her through a stride position (*d*), and the movement is continued to a stand (*e*, *f*, and *g*).

43*a*

43*b*

43*e*

43*f*

43c

43d

43g

This skill should be mastered before learning the back walkover.

# Back Walkover

**44.** The starting position (*a*) is stable and straight with the arms over the head. The weight is directly over the left leg, and there is a straight line from the left foot to the head. The right leg is extended with the pointed toe lightly touching the mat. In *b* the head drops back to start the movement. Control is important. The head is never thrown backward. The back walkover has to be made from one leg. The other leg is off the mat. The spotter helps to raise the right leg (and also supports the back).

The eyes look for the mat (*c*). The right leg continues to rise.

In *d* the hands make contact with the mat. As soon as the hands touch, the right leg kicks while the left leg pushes to get the hips up and over. Timing is important. The legs react just as the hands touch the mat.

A split-stride position is being passed through in *e*. In *f*, *g*, and *h* there is a stepping down to the standing position. Control is important. There is a stepdown—not a fall.

44*b*

44*c*

44*f*

44*g*

44a

44d

44e

44h

The back walkover should be learned well, because it lends itself so well to floor-exercise routines. This exercise allows a number of options. It can be carried out one-handed or with a switch of the legs.

# Backbend from One Leg

**45.** In the starting position (*a*) only one foot is in contact with the mat. Weight is balanced over the left leg with the body stretched and straight. In *b* the head drops back to start the movement. The right leg extends.

The basic principles of the walkover apply. The landing of the hands (*c*) is soft and controlled. The push-off of the left leg and the whip of the right leg begin just as the hands make contact with the mat. Through the handstand position (*d*). Stepdown (*e*) and the standing position (*f*).

45*a*

45*c*

45*d*

45*b*

45*e*

45*f*

# Gainer Back Walkover— Switch Leg to One Knee

Like many skills, this one can be carried out in different ways. For example, it could be done to a stand. Here, it is being done to one knee. Also, in this sequence the switch isn't necessary, but it is an attractive variation.

**46.** In *a*, the start in a poised position with the weight over the right foot. A forward movement (*b*). The arms are being used to build up momentum. By *c* the right leg has been positioned for a spring. The arms are ready to swing. The position in *d* results from all movements working together. There has been a spring off the right leg, a whip of the left leg, a movement of the arms, and an arch of the back. She is completely airborne in the back walkover position. The right is bent and ready to move to the landing, making for the switch.

In *e* the hands are on the mat, and the right leg is ready to land. Landing is on the knee with the left leg extended. The landing continues (*f*) so that she is sitting on the right heel. The left remains extended, and the arms are forward. In *g* a stag-sit pose position.

46a

46b

46e

46c

46d

46f

46g

# Valdez

**47.** A valdez is really a continuation of the back walkover skills. In *a*, a sitting position with the left leg bent and the right leg extended. The left leg becomes the push-off leg and the right leg the kick leg. Either hand could be on the mat, but it seems more attractive to have the hand opposite to the kick leg on the mat. The exact finger position is decided by comfort. Usually, the fingers point slightly away toward the wall, but differences among performers are not great—just a matter of degree.

In *b* the left leg has started its push and the right arm has started to swing upward and down. By *c* the right hand has reached the mat —right leg is extended upward—left leg has pushed off the mat and continues its motion. This is just about the back walkover position.

A stepping out of the back walkover position (*d* and *e*) to a stand.

The valdez can be varied. In the handstand position (*c*) the legs can be brought together.

47*a*

47*b*

47*d*

47c

47e

47f

# Back Walkover to a Split

The unique aspect of this skill is that the back walkover takes you directly to a split. There is no preliminary landing on one foot before the split.

**48.** A good stretch position in *a*. The first movements (*b* and *c*) are like those of a regular back walkover. From *d* on, the performance becomes different. The use of the arms becomes important—so in this series we'll think of a right-handed performer. Control is needed, and the spotter helps. The weight has to be shifted to the right hand so that the left hand can be lifted from the mat.

At *e* the weight has shifted to the right hand. In *f* the left hand has moved out of the way to make room for the right leg to move through to a split. The hips keep moving forward so that they end up near the hands. It's really a complete rotation over the right arm. If done well, and the right leg reaches forward, the hips should land near the right hand.

48a

48b

48e

48f

48c

48d

48g

48h

# Back Handspring

**49.** No one, in learning the back handspring, should attempt to carry out the full skill. It is not natural to jump backward. You have gradually to get used to the idea. So you start by carrying out only the first part, and with a spotter present. From the starting position (*a*) the knees bend to the position shown in *b*. Photo *b* is important. You've got to be off balance and actually falling backward. Trunk remains fairly erect. From this position the legs spring and the arms swing. There is no attempt to carry out a full handspring. The jump is back toward the spotter.

49*a*

**50.** A backspring is made with a spotter. Sometimes two spotters are used. A spotting belt can be used for safety, but learning is better when there is a spotter. In *a* the bend of the legs is starting. A good off-balance position is reached in *b*. This is a position that cannot be held. The upper body is straight. The arms are starting their upward swing. By *c* the backward spring, the arm action, and the arch of the back have brought her near the handstand position. Vision is on the hands as they are about to touch the mat. The legs are ready to move up through handstand position. In *d* the hands push, and the legs snap down. In *e*, up to a standing position.

Spotting is on both the back and the legs.

50*a*

50*d*

49b

49c

50b

50c

50e

**51.** Carrying out the back handspring without spotting. In *a*, a start from an erect position. The arms do not have to be above the head. It's a matter of choice. In *b*, leaning back with the legs bent. Arms are ready for a full swing. The legs have just finished their extension in *c*. The head is going back with the arms—never before the arms. In *d*, just past the handstand position. The hands will push, and the legs will snap down. When the feet touch (*e*), the body is already almost erect. The standing position (*f*).

51*a*

51*d*

51b

51c

51e

51f

# Back Handspring Walkout

**52.** If the landing from the handspring is on one foot it is usually easier and smoother to go on to the next skills. The preparation for the handspring (*a* and *b*). As the hands touch (*c*), the legs are being brought to stride position. The right leg lands (*d*), and she rises to a position with the weight on one foot and the other pointed forward (*e*).

52*a*

52*c*

52b

52d

52e

# Forward Roll to a Back Handspring

**53.** An effective and attractive way to get to a back handspring is from a forward roll. The roll is being carried out in *a*, *b*, *c*, and *d*. The roll continues only to the off-balance position (*e*). In *f* the arms are being thrown up and back, and the legs begin their push. Head moves with the arms. The handstand position (*g*).

Photo *h* shows clearly that the hands are off the mat before the feet hit. By the time the landing is made (*i*) the body is already fairly erect with the arms almost overhead. From this position she could continue to another back handspring.

53*c*

53*d*

53*g*

53*h*

53*a*

53*b*

53*e*

53*f*

53*i*

53*j*

# Roundoff to Back Handspring

**54.** The back handspring can follow easily and smoothly from a roundoff. The hurdle (*a*). Start of the cartwheel (*b*). The left hand has landed (*c*). In *d* the body is turning. As the feet land (*e*) the body has momentum. In *f* the body is still moving, and the take-off for the backspring will take place when the off-balance position is reached. By *g* the hands touch, and the legs are swinging upward. Photo *h* shows that the hands have completed their push with the feet still in the air.

In learning this skill it's best to have an experienced spotter.

54*a*

54*d*

54*g*

54*h*

54b

54c

54e

54f

54i

54j

## Standing Back Somie

**55.** The mechanics of this skill should be
learned well before it is combined with others.
In *a*, a standing position with the arms over
the head. The spotter has a hand on the
gymnast's back. The leg bend (*b*). The body is
balanced directly over the feet. The arms are
positioned to swing. In *c* the legs are springing
and the arms are swinging upward. The jump
is straight up. The tuck position is started
and the head is thrown back only after there
has been full extension of the legs at take-off. In
*d* you can see the fine height that has been
attained. The knees have been pulled toward
the chest. Vision is on the floor so that she will
know when to open from the tuck and land.
Landing (*e*), and an erect position (*f*).

An experienced spotter is important to learning
the skill. A belt is often used, but a good
spotter can do more than the belt in that she
can help control the legs.

It's important to distinguish between the
techniques of the somie and the back
handspring. In the back handspring the body is
kept fairly low—almost a "slinky" movement.
In contrast, the somie is an effort to get
height. It starts from a balanced position.

55*a*

55*d*

55*b*

55*c*

55*e*

55*f*

# DANCE POSITIONS

## Ballet Positions

The ballet is related to gymnastics in that both try to communicate through graceful and elegant movement. Ballet has pleased many generations throughout the world. The grace and beauty that has come from ballet should certainly be added to the gymnast's performance. And it's not necessary to be a ballerina to borrow from ballet. The five basic positions are important to a fine gymnastics performance. Not only do these positions actually appear in the routine, they influence nearly all gymnastic skills. The better the five basic positions are learned, the better you will perform. They are seldom learned quickly, because they do require practice and flexibility. It's a good idea to include them in your warm-up exercises.

Of course, good posture is always important, but special attention is given to the positions of the feet and arms. The feet present their most attractive picture when the toes are turned outward. The arms are rounded. The elbows are slightly bent, and the wrists and hands are an extension of the curve made by the arms. The carryover from the basic arm positions can make almost any routine a prettier one.

**56.** The basic ballet positions are shown from left to right.

**First position.** The heels are together, and the toes are out. With the toes pointed outward it is easier to move to the side. The arms are rounded, as they are in the other positions.

**Second position.** The heels are somewhat apart, but the toes are still pointing outward. The arm position is significant, because it is one of grace when running to start a skill.

**Third position.** The heel of the front foot is brought to the middle of the arch of the other foot. The toes are pointed outward. The knees are squeezed together. One arm is up and the other to the side.

**Fourth position.** The right foot is slid forward. Weight is equally over both legs. Toes are turned out. It's a good position to start various turns. One arm remains up and the other is lowered.

**Fifth position.** Heel to toe—toe to heel. The front heel touches one toe, and the front toe almost touching the back heel. There is as much turnout of the toes as flexibility allows. Both arms are overhead.

# Waltz Step

**57.** A very good connector between tumbling skills. The waltz is very flexible in that it can be carried out in a straight line, turning, or forward and backward. The waltz step is often called a "down-up-up." That means that the first step is started on the flat of the foot (*b*), and the next two on the toes (*c* and *d*). In *e* and *f* the left foot is making solid contact.

The next two steps (*g* and *h*) are carried out on the toes. The pattern makes for a graceful up and down movement of the body.

The arms move in relation to the opposite leg. When the right leg is moving forward, the left arm circles. The right arm moves with the left leg.

57*a*

57*b*

57*e*

57*f*

57*c*

57*d*

57*g*

57*h*

# Chassé

**58.** A good dance skill for going from one move to another. The arms are in the second position. Both legs are turned outward. Other ballet positions are seen. The lead leg is "chased" but never quite caught. The arms remain in the second position throughout the entire chassé.

58a

58d

59b

58b

58c

## Pas de Bourrée

**59.** A pleasing way to go from one pose to another or to use between skills. It can be carried out sideways or turning in place. As in the waltz the "down-up-up" idea holds. In *a* the left foot is solidly placed. The next step (*b*) is made on the toe of the right foot and in *c* on the ball of the left foot. In *d* once more there is a solid foot position, but on the right foot.

59a

59c

59d

## Assemblé

**60.** In this step the feet gather together for possibly a jump. It is often used after a fast tumbling skill in which you are on one foot. In *b* the right leg is kicked out to the side while the left leg stays down. In *c* a landing to the fifth position with the right foot in front. From this plié position there can be a jump or a pose.

60*a*

61*b*

61*c*

60b

60c

## Stride Leap

**61.** In *a*, the running approach. The take-off (*b*) is being made with a bent leg. It could be made with the lead leg straight. The arms are starting to drive upward to increase the amount of lift. In *c* the right leg extends, and the take-off leg is brought up. The trunk is erect in a balanced position. Upon landing (*d*) movement continues.

61a

61d

61e

## Stag Leap

**62.** In *a*, a running approach. The take-off (*b*) is made with the weight balanced over the jumping foot. The lead leg is already bent. Good height is seen in *c*. The trail leg is extended and turned outward. In *d* the landing is soft and under control.

62*a*

62*d*

62b

62c

62e

62f

## Tours Jeté

**63.** Here, the start is with a chassé (*a*, *b*, and *c*). Arms are in the second position. In *d*, preparation for the spring. The arms are brought back so that they can swing to add to the lift. The take-off (*e*). The left leg is extended and swung in the direction of the run. In *f*, the turn in the air. Arms are in the fifth position.

The turn completely reverses the direction of the body. As she is about to land (*g*) the right leg points directly backward—that is, in the same direction that the left leg was pointing in at take-off. In *h* the arms have been opened to the second position.

63*a*

63*b*

63*e*

63*f*

63c

63d

63g

63h

## Cat Leap

**64.** A chassé (*a*, *b*, and *c*) is a good way to get ready for the cat leap. In *d*, a strong take-off position with the left leg solidly planted. The right leg has been bent (*e*) during the lift. It is straightening as the left leg starts to bend. Landing (*f*) is on the right foot.

In the air the knees are bent in turn. During the bending each knee is turned slightly out.

64*a*

64*b*

64*e*

64*f*

64c

64d

64g

64h

## Hitch Kick

**65.** The now familiar chassé approach
(*a* and *b*) and readiness (*c*) for a lift from the
right leg. In *d* the extended left kicks upward.
While in the air the legs change positions so that
the landing (*e*) is on the left foot with the
right leg extended.

This skill is similar to the cat leap except that
the legs remain extended during the exchange.

65*a*

65*d*

65*e*

65b

65c

65f

65g

## Seat-Tuck Jump

**66.** A jump is from both feet (a leap is from one foot). The assemblé (*a*, *b*, and *c*) is one good way to get into jumping position. Getting into good position for the jump is as important as the jump itself. In the air (*d*) the legs are tucked toward the seat. The landing (*e*) is soft with the arms in the second position.

66a

66d

66e

## Arched-Back Jump

**67.** The back is arched and the feet tucked to make for a graceful jump. As in all take-offs from both feet, both the movement into jumping position and the landing have to be carried out smoothly and gracefully.

66b

66c

67a

67b

## Jump Full Turn to Knee Spin

**68.** An assemblé to get to jumping position (*d*). In (*e*), a turn in the air. She could simply land on two feet, but in this series two dance skills are combined. The landing (*f*) is on the right leg, and she will bring her left knee to the mat. The turn starts to the left and will continue that way. Spin is on the left knee (*g*) and then switches to the right knee (*h*). Finish is in a kneeling lunge position (*i*).

68a

68d

68e

68b

68c

68f

68g

68h

68i

# Arabesque Turn

**69.** In *a* weight is on the right foot with the left foot extended. By *c* weight has moved to the left toe, and the right foot is pushing to create the turning movement. The arabesque position is shown in *d*. Weight is on one leg with the other extended in back. Arm position can vary, but usually one arm is high and the other low. Finish is in a pose (*e*). Though this turn is being made in the arabesque position, many other positions could be used for this single leg turn.

*69a*

*69b*

*69d*

*69c*

*69e*

# POSES

Poses are never held very long. They are brief pauses. They are like punctuation marks in a composition, and can form a brief interval between skills. As soon as a pose is struck, it's time to move on to another skill.

There are standing poses and low-level poses. Both types are needed.

Not all poses are taken from ballet, but many do use at least parts of ballet positions. In standing poses the toes are usually pointed outward, and the arms are often curved. In general, it is more graceful to have the weight on one leg and the other extended with pointed toe.

All in all, poses are a matter of creativity. The variety of poses is only limited by the imagination.

70a

70b

70c

70d

# COMBINATIONS

In looking at some of the skills in tumbling, the dance, and poses, we've already linked some of them together in combinations. Each individual skill is fun to do, and the mastery of a skill brings satisfaction. But the gymnast knows that the greatest satisfaction is in putting together the various skills to compose a full routine.

To show complete routines would defeat our very purpose. Routines should be the product of imagination and creativity. That's the fascination of gymnastics. Perhaps no two optional routines should ever be entirely

## From One Split to Another

**71.** Any girl who can do a good split should use it in combinations, because this show of flexibility is highly attractive. A split (*a*). The movement forward (*b*) with the right arm lifted and the left hand on the mat. The left leg is going to be lifted so that it's behind the head. The right arm will come forward so that she can roll over the right shoulder. A push away from the mat and the left leg will be pushed back. A push back and a finish in another split.

71*a*

## Swedish Fall to a Split

**72.** In *a*, a scale position, and in *b*, the fall to almost a push-off position. The supporting leg and the shoulders are in a straight line. The free leg is straight and pointing toward the ceiling. The landing is soft and under control. From *b* to *c* the right leg is crossed back toward the wall. The right arm pushes off and is brought upward. A split position appears in 71*c*.

72*a*

alike. Personality should express itself. Good gymnastics has to be a happy wedding of discipline and the free creative spirit.

While it would not be right to specify complete routines, we can recognize that there is a natural linking between various skills. They just go well with each other. For this reason some combinations are suggested. Others are possible and could even be better. Again, a few of the infinite number of combinations are presented. You may too decide to use many others—as surely you should—but the following combinations might be useful to you, at least for a time.

71b

71c

72b

72c

## Pike Back Roll, Seat Spin, Pose

**73.** The use of simple skills to create a pleasing combination. The start (*a*) is with a simple pose (others could be used). In *b*, ready for a pike back roll. In *d* the landing from the roll is on the knees in a swan position. A roll to the side (*e*) with the right leg extended and up. This pose is held only briefly. From there (*f*) a seat spin. In *g* there is a modified V seat. The legs are exchanged (*h*) so that left leg is extended. Weight is on the right knee. Next (*i*) a kneeling lunge position.

73*a*

73*d*

73*e*

*73b*

*73c*

*73f*

*73g*

*73h*

*73i*

# Dance into Back Walkover

**74.** A pose (*a*). Chassé with the arms circling (*b*). In *c*, arabesque position with the arms out to the side. Two steps to the right foot and ready for the back walkover (*d*). The back walkover (*e* and *f*). Lunge (*g*), and back to a pose (*h*).

74*a*

74*b*

74*e*

74*f*

74c

74d

74g

74h

## Cartwheel, Hitch-Kick,
## Front Walkover

**75.** A pose (*a*), pas de bourrée completed (*b*), and ready to step in the cartwheel (*c*). In *d*, a one-handed cartwheel, and in *e*, out of the cartwheel. The hitch-kick (*f*) to a front walkover (*g*). In the middle of the front walkover (*h*). A step forward (*i*) to a pose position (*j*).

75*a*

75*d*

75*e*

75*h*

75b

75c

75f

75g

75i

75j

## Using Some Simple Skills to Form a Fluid Combination

**76.** Posed position (*a*). A cross turn with the arms in the high fifth position (*b*). Left leg kicked out to start the cartwheel (*c*). In the cartwheel (*d*). Left-handed lunge (*e*). A graceful rock back on the right leg (*f*) to a handstand (*g*). Tucking of the head to do the forward roll (*h*). Finish of the forward roll (*i*) and another forward roll (*j*). Finish of the roll in a straddle position (*k*). A roll back to the shoulders (*l*). Both legs will circle to the left side. The right knee bent and a sitting side position (*m*). In *n* the left leg is folded back—a pose.

76c          76d          76e

76i          76j          76k

76a

76b

76f

76g

76h

76l

76m

76n

# THE ROUTINE

We've been looking at a few combinations of skills. The number of possible combinations is almost infinite. Yet, as suggested, certain combinations are indicated because there is a natural linking between certain skills. We can extend the notion of combinations, putting them together to form the routine. The contents of a routine is also limited only by the imagination. Yet it is useful to say a few things about the routine.

*Music.* As you know, only one instrument is allowed. It's usually a piano, and for practical purposes often a record or tape is used. Music should be appropriate. This means that it should suit both your personality and the nature of your routine. Everyone's personality is different, so you will have a feel for the music that's best for you. All good routines include a change of pace—so the music should have a change of tempo.

*Difficulties.* Routines do include a certain number of difficult skills. These difficulties should not be concentrated together. Instead, they should be well distributed throughout the routine. Also, they should be distributed so that they take place in various parts of the floor.

*Level.* Some skills are performed on your feet and others with the body close to the mat. Both types should be included.

*Floor area.* All the space should be used. Exercises are never crammed into one spot; they range over the entire floor. Even when moving from one corner to another, it's best not to use a beeline. A circular path is better. It adds interest.

*Facial expression.* A pleasant facial expression is always good, but expressions should not be forced. They should appear natural and appropriate to what you are doing. When you do make an error and feel upset about it, don't show it.

*Your skills.* Along the way there will be skills at which you will be very good. There will be others that you haven't quite mastered. *Try* to master all skills. But in putting together your routine include only those skills at which you are very good.

*Endurance.* A good routine creates the impression that the performer could continue forever. There is no appearance of fatigue. The fine gymnast practices and builds up stamina so that she can carry out her routine three times in a row. In this way the gymnast performs better and receives the great health benefits that gymnastics has to offer.

# *Balance Beam*

## ABOUT THE BALANCE BEAM

Balance! The word probably means much to you already. For example, balance is used to describe our newly strengthened concern with our natural environment—good ecology depends on a balance in nature. Balance becomes a needed word in talking about many things in life including our economic system. Balance is always important to us.

But for now we are interested in balance as it relates to human movement. The fine athlete and the graceful dancer are always balanced. Balance makes for beauty of action. It seems that we have always sensed the pleasing and satisfying effects produced by balance. Thus, even though the balance beam as we now have it is relatively new, the techniques involved have their beginnings in the basics of human movement.

When the balance beam came into widespread use for formal competition, it had to be standardized. The dimensions of the official beam were set as follows:

> *Length*—5 meters, or 16 feet 4 inches
> *Width on top*—10 centimeters, or about 4 inches
> *Height*—120 centimeters, or about 4 feet
> *Thickness*—16 centimeters, or 6½ inches.

Most schools and sports organizations will have commercially made beams. This usually insures accuracy. But many great performers started with homemade beams, built with the help of either parents or students.

*What can be done on the balance beam?* Nearly everything that can be done in floor exercise. Of course, there is the practical limitation that the beam is only four inches wide. This reality is somewhat restricting, but the great performer makes it appear that she has all the room in the world.

The routine on the beam is made up of the spectacular and graceful movements of tumbling and the dance. All of these movements blend together in a way that is pleasing to the viewer and satisfying to the performer. In this book we will be showing many of the skills that can be put together for a good composition. We cannot include everything that can be done, because there are so many possible skills that can be carried out. The possibilities are only limited by imagination and the work that accompanies ambition.

*Time and scoring.* Both could change, so you have to look at the newest rule book. At the moment, the time limit is between one minute and twenty seconds to one minute and forty-five seconds. As for scoring, there are specific guidelines for the judges. We won't list them here, but in general the judges look for "elements of difficulty" and execution. An even performance and rhythm are important. In general, a performance that you feel is good will get a good score. But do check the rules for scoring with your coach.

## OUR APPROACH

Your experience in learning the balance beam is bound to be enjoyable and satisfying. And there will be lasting rewards in grace, poise, and confidence. Though there is lots of fun along the way, it takes hard work to get good. It also takes intelligence.

The goal, of course, is a pleasing composition that brings satisfaction to you and delight to the viewers. All compositions, whether in writing, music, or gymnastics, are made up of various elements that are blended together. So the first job is to master the elements. Nearly all the allotted time on the beam will be spent in combining *tumbling* and *dance movements*. Hence, we will be giving a lot of attention to these elements. But a routine has to have a start and a finish. It's necessary to start by getting up on the beam and finally to get off it to complete the routine. So we will be looking at the techniques of the *mount* and the *dismount*. Actually, since the mount starts things off, we ought to look at it first. And, because you know that you must eventually leave the beam, we will be spending some time on the dismount.

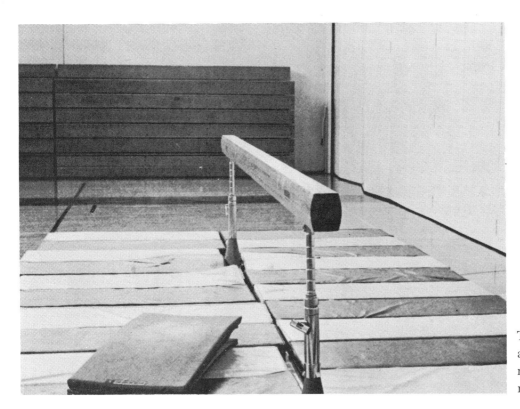

The beam, the arrangement of mats, and the reuther board.

The gymnast takes an interest in equipment. She is ready to set it up or put it away.

All sports activities have their merits, and nearly all of them offer great health benefits. But in all sports there are *safety precautions*. Thus it is with the balance beam, and you will surely agree that we ought to talk about safety.

Your *warm-up*: in all sports activity the warm-up is an important part of the day's workout, and no fine athlete ever neglects it. Since the warm-up comes first each day, we'll give it early attention.

The ingredients are put together logically and naturally to form *combinations*. Because there are so many possible combinations, we will only illustrate with a couple. Lastly, we will be talking about your *routine*. The best thing we can do is to talk about the tips that performers and coaches have found to be most helpful.

*Progression* is a familiar word in teaching and learning. It means, of course, that one learns the simplest things first and then goes on to the more complex. Seems reasonable enough. But we can't be entirely sure about progression. What might seem a simple skill may be difficult for some girls, and what looks like a difficult skill may be quickly learned by others. But we have made an effort to present skills from easiest to more difficult.

## SAFETY

All sports involve a certain amount of risk. The football player can get hurt, the runner can pull a muscle, the basketball player can receive a knee injury, and so it goes. Actually, there are relatively few injuries to gymnasts, but the goal is to have no injuries at all.

Equipment has to be sound. A commercial beam is highly reliable. Placement of mats is important. The mats should be on both sides of the beam. And when working on dismounts, there should be mats off both ends of the beam.

Start on the floor—then on a low beam. As you get better, you will progress to the high beam.

Learn how to handle a fall. If you do this, a fall can be completely harmless.

Wait for your instructor before getting on the beam. It's much safer to have the instructor with you.

When a new or difficult skill is tried, the instructor should be on hand to spot you.

All in all, the dangers aren't that great, but surely you'll agree that reasonable precautions should be taken.

# GETTING STARTED

The balance beam holds a natural fascination, and nearly all girls take to it quite readily. As in all skills, there is variation in learning speed. Some girls take quickly to the beam. Others need more time to get to the same level of skill. There are some general hints about getting started that will prove useful to most girls:

1. A start can be made on a line placed on the floor or, even better, a very low beam—perhaps one placed on the floor. In this way there will be no problems of mounting and dismounting. You can simply step on and off the beam. And, of course, there is no fear of falling.

2. Floor exercise should come first. Many of the skills of floor exercise are used on the beam, but it's better to learn these skills on the floor before trying them on the beam.

3. Attractive walking habits should be learned right away. The upper body is kept firm to avoid wobble. The legs swing freely. Arms are in a soft position.

4. Walk a lot on the beam. It gives you confidence, and you get to feel that the beam is a "mile wide."

5. The head should be kept up with vision directed toward the end of the beam. Try not to look directly down.

6. When you can try the beam at full height, learn the simplest of the mounts and dismounts.

7. A good spotter is needed. She is there to help you. But try to do some things by yourself. You have to "solo" to build confidence.

8. When learning new skills try them on a line drawn on the floor or on a low beam. Then take them to the high beam.

9. The beam often requires a different tempo for the skills. They have to be carried out more slowly. For example, a forward roll is carried out quickly on the floor, but on the beam the action is slower and more controlled.

10. From time to time you will fall off the beam. Expect it, and learn to fall safely.

## YOUR WARM-UP

If facilities and scheduling permit, the gymnast will usually have worked on other events before turning to the balance beam. In this case the warm-up will have already been carried out. But if the beam is the first event of the day, a thorough warm-up is needed before going to it.

Even if your first event of the workout for the day is not the balance beam, the beam itself can be most helpful in getting a good warm-up. With that in mind some warm-up exercises are shown. The exercises shown are only a few of the many possibilities.

## YOUR ROUTINE ON THE BEAM

You've learned some individual skills, and you've learned to combine some of them. Next, of course, you'll want to extend the combinations to form a routine. That's the way you enter and enjoy competition. Naturally, your routines will become more sophisticated as you master more and more skills. Along the way there are some useful things to keep in mind while composing and carrying out your routine:

1. The whole beam should be used. This doesn't mean that you just go from one end to the other. For example, you may move to the center of the beam, turn to come back, and then turn again to go to the other end. In other words the entire beam should be used, but not in a monotonous way.

2. Mounts and dismounts should be at about the same skill level. It detracts if one is simple and the other complicated.

3. For the most part it's best to use the skills that you can carry out well, but don't confine the routine to difficulties in one category. For example, it won't do to be expert in the dance and ignore tumbling. Learn all areas so that the performance will be even.

4. Make the routine interesting to watch. There should be a good change of level from high to low. Beginners have a tendency to concentrate on low-level skills.

5. A change in tempo is attractive. The skills should be carried out at differing speeds.

6. Vision is generally directed toward the end of the beam and in some

skills directly at the beam. But do include skills where your gaze can be directed toward the judges and audience.

7. Facial expression is highly important but somewhat difficult to talk about. To a great extent facial expression has to depend on your own personality. But a few things can be said. Expression has to be pleasant— yet it shouldn't be artificial or forced. Smiles are best when you feel like smiling—usually, when you are doing a fun stunt on the beam that you do well and enjoy doing. In any case, feelings of strain or failure should not be expressed on the face. After all, one of the great arts of gymnastics is to make the difficult look easy and comfortable.

8. You really have to expect to fall off the beam from time to time. Beginners fall often, and even the fine performers have a fall now and then. A fall is rarely disastrous, but it is the time to keep cool and calm. Don't try to rush back on the beam. Wait a second and take a deep breath. It gives you time to think. In getting back on the beam, there are two important things to remember. Get back smoothly and quickly. Don't try for a formal mount. And when you get back on the beam, do not repeat the trick that you have missed. Instead, go on to the next part of your routine.

# Warm-Up

**1.** The hamstrings (muscles in the back of the thighs) are being stretched (*a*). Also, the shoulders are being stretched. The movement is a bouncing one. In *b*, a good stretch of the back and stomach muscles. With the hands on the beam the hips move forward. In *c*, a familiar warm-up for those who have been in dance classes. A good stretch for the legs and also a good lateral stretch for the body.

An excellent exercise for the trunk and lower legs (*d*). Splits are highly important in gymnastics (*e*). Flexibility is needed for many movements.

The balance beam makes a good prop for a good warm-up for all events.

1*a*

1*d*

1b

1c

1e

# Front Support Mount

**2.** The gymnast faces the beam in *a*. Hands are at her side. In *b* hands are on the beam and there is a jump to the front support position. The distance between hands is about shoulder width. The right leg swings over the beam in *c*. Now you can see why the close spacing of the hands is important. The right arm is not in the way of the swinging leg. In *d*, a straddle sit on the beam. The movement is smooth and continuous with a gentle landing. After the landing on the beam a number of movements can be carried out. The arms are being brought over the head in *e*, and the body remains in a straight line. In *f*, a movement to a V seat. The hands move to the beam, and the legs are raised. This movement is more effective if the legs remain straight while it is being carried out.

There are various options from this position. For example, one foot can be placed on the beam, allowing movement to a standing position.

The front support mount is one of the simplest and one of the first to be learned.

2a

2d

2e

2b

2c

2f

## Stag or Knee Mount

**3.** Just as in the previous mount, a position is taken facing the beam (*a*). In *b* the hands are placed on the beam about shoulder width, and the right leg is kicked to the beam. Left leg is downward. Both legs are straight. The position is very stable. There is a push of the right leg and the body weight is taken by the hands (*c*). The hips are lifted so that the left leg can be pulled up on the beam in a kneeling position. In *d* the arms are raised, and there is a stag kneeling position.

3*a*

3*d*

4*a*

4*b*

3b

3c

## Scissor-Kick Vault Mount

**4.** The approach to the beam is from an angle (*a*). It could be from either side, according to personal preference. You will notice that the take-off is from a reuther board. This board helps you to get height, and you will be using it for various mounts. The lift off the board is from the outside foot. Spotting is relatively easy. The spotter grasps both the upper arm and wrist. In this case the gymnast's left arm is swinging freely. However, when learning, it is easier to place the left hand on the beam, and this hand placement is considered perfectly acceptable.

In *b* the left leg is kicked upward and ready for a landing on the beam. The height of the lift has brought the hips above the beam. The landing has been made on the left foot (*c*). The right leg remains straight and has been swung forward. In *d* the right leg has been tucked, and the arms take a diagonal position.

4c

4d

## Single-Knee Mount

**5.** The beam is faced in *a*. Hands are placed on the beam (*b*). The distance between hands is about shoulder width. In *c* the arms and leg action have lifted the hips high enough that the right knee can be placed on the beam between the arms. Body weight is really to the side of the knee. The left arm and left leg are lifted to a posed position (*d*). Movement out of the posed position will be made immediately.

5*a*

5*d*

## Wolf- or Stag-Vault Mount

**6.** This is a half-squat, half-straddle mount. In *a* the reuther board is placed close to the beam. Approach is short (*b*). In *c* hands are placed on the beam. The leg drive is from both legs. The gymnast tries to lift straight up. Good height has been attained in *d*. The right leg is moving to the side. The left knee is coming forward with the toes curled so that the foot can be placed on the beam. The hands take

6*b*

6*c*

5b

5c

the weight of the body. The right leg has swung to the side, and the left knee is coming through between the arms. A briefly held pose ( *e* ).

When this skill is first learned, spotting is important. The spotter stands on the other side of the beam opposite the reuther board. The jobs of the spotter are to assist with height and to keep the gymnast from going past the beam.

6a

6d

6e

# Straddle-Vault Mount to Japanese Split

**7.** The approach is perpendicular to the beam (*a*). The reuther board is used. The take-off from the reuther board is from both feet (*b*). The hands are moving toward the beam. Fingers are forward. Distance between hands is shoulder width. The legs are beginning to straddle in *c*. The high position of the hips is needed to get the feet on the beam. Feet are on the beam in *d*, and the straddle mount is completed. Though the straddle mount really has been completed, the Japanese split (*e*) makes a graceful and effective next move. In *f* toes are pointed, and the arms placed upward.

*7a*

*7b*

7c

7d

7e

7f

## Tuck-Vault Mount

**8.** The approach is at right angles to the beam (*a*). The reuther board is used. The approach is short—only a few steps (*b*). In *c*, a two-footed take-off from the reuther board. The hands are placed on the beam at shoulder width. Hips attain height toward the "back" or approach side of the beam in *d*. This makes it possible for the feet to come through and onto the beam. Correct hip height and position depends on a take-off that is straight upward. You can see that the placing of the feet on the beam is a controlled action. The feet are closely spaced and the knees are together in *e*. The arms are lifting. A briefly held posed position (*f*). In general, you go "through" a pose rather than hold it at all.

8a

8d

8e

8b

8c

8f

## Flank Vault to Stride Position

**9.** Approach is perpendicular to the beam (*a*). A reuther board is used. The spotter is positioned to assist. In *b*, a take-off from both feet. Hands are being placed on the beam. The needed hip height is attained in *c*. Body weight is shifted to the left hand so that the right arm can make way for the swinging left leg. The spotter offers support. Notice that it is the left leg that is going to swing to the beam. It would be easier to put the right leg on the beam, but the use of the left leg makes for an interesting variation.

In *d* the left leg has cleared the beam and is ready to land. In *e* the left leg is on the beam, and right leg is downward. An extended body position with one leg forward and the other down appears in *f*.

9*c*

9*d*

9a

9b

9e

9f

## Single-Leg Step-up on End of Beam

**10.** The approach is made from the end of the beam. A reuther board is used. The spotter holds the upper arm of the gymnast and makes the approach with her (*a*). Ready for a strong take-off from one leg in *b*. You can see the placing of the reuther board in relation to the end of the beam—also the distance of the take-off foot from the beam. There has to be enough room for the lead leg to swing freely and reach the beam. In *c* the take-off leg is now fully extended, and the left foot is moving forward to be placed on the beam. Spotting supplies lift and aids balance. The left foot is on the beam, and the right leg is extended downward (*d*). In *e*, extension; in *f*, pose.

10*a*

10*d*

10*e*

10*b*

10*c*

10*f*

## Chest-Stand Mount to Lever

**11.**   The gymnast stands close to the beam and faces it in *a*. She will put her hands on the beam and jump hard. The spotter is on the other side of the beam. A hard jump results in the needed hip height (*b*). Though the upper body is in contact with the beam, the body weight is supported by the arms. Legs are extended upward in *c*. The legs could be tucked, but it is more attractive to have them straight.

The most critical part of the skill is seen in *d*. The right elbow takes the body weight, and the elbow is against the stomach to form the lever. Legs are in the straddle position to aid balance. The lowering of the legs is very controlled. The legs lower so as to straddle the beam. The head rises (*e*). During these movements balance is over the right arm. It is important to use the right arm as a lever so that the lowering of the legs can be slow and controlled. In *f*, the straddle position on the beam. Through a pose (*g*).

11*a*

11*d*

11*e*

11b

11c

11f

11g

## Forward-Roll Vault Mount

**12.** The approach is from the end of the beam (*a*). A reuther board is used. The take-off is from both feet. Hands are along the beam with the thumbs on top (*b*). The spotter is ready to help with hip height. The spotter now helps with hip height (*c*). The gymnast's head is starting to come under, and has come all the way under in *d*. There is a good pike position. Some beginners find it necessary to

put the hands under the beam to increase stability. If the hands do go under the beam, there is a fraction of a point deduction. Yet in the early stages this hand position can be helpful; it can prevent a fall.

In *e* the roll continues. The spotter is ready to help continue the roll in *f*. The roll ends in a standing position (*g*). By *h* the performer is ready for the next skill.

12*a*

12*b*

12*e*

12*f*

12c

12d

12g

12h

# Handstand Vault Mount

**13.** Here the approach is at right angles to the center of the beam (*a*), but the same mount (using the English grip) can be carried out at the end of the beam. The run is full so that good height can be obtained from the drive off the reuther board. Two spotters are standing by. In *b* hips are high. The hands reach the beam with the arms fairly straight—the straighter the better. The spotter is helping with height. By *c* the upper body and hips are directly above the beam. The legs are piked and straddled. The hips must be above the beam before the legs are extended. The straddle position of the legs makes extension easier. In *d* the legs are finishing their extension and coming together. Handstand position (*e*). From here there are various options including the cartwheel and reverse press. We will be talking about them in the section on tumbling.

It's useful to have two spotters. One helps with height, and the other is prepared to keep the gymnast from going past the vertical position. You can see that it is best if the spotters are fairly tall. Often spotters are members of the boys' team.

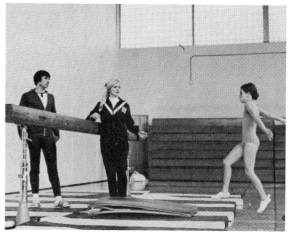

13*a*

13*d*

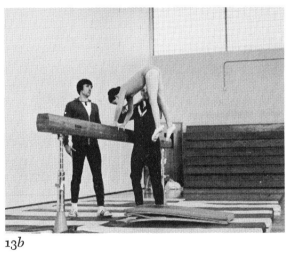

13b

13c

13e

# Walks

**14.** In the dip walk (*a*), the leg is in contact with the beam bends. The other leg is extended so that the foot dips below the top of the beam. In *b*, a straight step, and in *c*, the kick walk. Turning of the body (*d*). Sideward steps appear in *e* and *f*. In *g*, backward steps, and in *h*, backward steps with a different position of the arms. Steps to a pose (*i*).

14*a*

14*d*

14*e*

14*h*

14*i*

14b

14c

14f

14g

Walking may seem to be a simple activity, but
on the beam there are many ways of making
the walk more interesting and attractive.

## Hops and Runs

**15.** Both hops and runs can be effective ways of moving along the beam. In hops you land on the take-off foot. In runs you push from one foot and land on the other.

15*a*

15*d*

15*e*

15*h*

15*i*

15b

15c

15f

15g

# Waltz Step

**16.** Carried out on the beam, the waltz step can be looked upon as an interesting variation of the walk. The familiar "One . . . two-three," a long step followed by two shorter ones, makes for a change in tempo.

16a

16b

16e

16f

16c

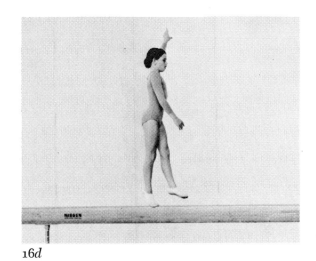

16d

16g

## Stride Leap

**17.**  The stride leap is a spectacular and
somewhat difficult skill. It has to start with a
powerful spring from one leg. The other leg
drives forward and up. The legs are apart to
form the stride position at maximum height.
Balance is needed. Balance and precision are
both needed for an effective landing on the beam.

17a

17b

17e

17f

17c

17d

17g

17h

## Assemblé—Tuck Jump

**18.** Weight is on the right leg in *a*, with left toe pointed forward. In *b* weight shifts to the left leg and the right leg swings forward. Descending from a leap in the air (*c*). Both feet are landing at about the same time. In *d*, assembling for a spring upward. The jump (*e*). Coming down (*f*). The tuck has already been made. The ending (*g*) is in a tuck position on the beam.

18*a*

18*b*

18*e*

18*f*

18c

18d

18g

# Chassé and Cat Leap

**19.** Left leg is forward in *a*, with weight on the right leg. In *b*, a stepping out to the left foot. In *c* the right foot chases (the meaning of chassé) the left foot but doesn't quite catch it. Landing (*d*) is on the right foot with the left extended. Weight on the left foot (*e*) and ready for the leap. In *f* the left leg extends for the spring and the right knee comes up. The left knee comes up as the right leg lowers (*g*). The legs switch positions. Landing will be on the right foot. In *h*, a stepping forward to the left foot. A pose (*i*).

19*c*

19*d*

19*g*

19*h*

19*a*

19*b*

19*e*

19*f*

19*i*

# Hitch-Kick

**20.** The left leg is free in *a* because the body weight is supported by the right leg. In *b* the left leg steps out. The left leg is planted and poised to spring (*c*).

The right leg kicks upward as the left leg springs (*d*). The arms move upward to get additional height. In *e* the left leg is now forward. There has been a switch of the legs— a hitch-kick. Landing is on the right leg (*f*). In *g*, a step forward. Pose (*h*).

20*a*

20*b*

20*e*

20*f*

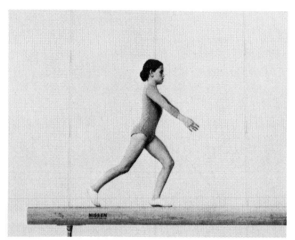

20c

20d

20g

20h

## Two-Footed Pivot, Standing

**21.** Start is on the left foot with the right foot pointed forward (*a*). In *b* weight has shifted to the right foot and the left foot has been brought forward so that the feet are close together. Up to the balls of the feet to make the turn in *c*. The left heel will lower to the beam after *d*. Finishing up with a pose (*e*).

21*a*

21*d*

21*e*

22*b*

22*c*

21b

21c

## Two-Footed Pivot—
## Squat Position

**22.** Weight is on the right foot with the left foot pointed forward (*a*). In *b* a step is taken. The distance between the feet should not be too great. A moderate distance will give more control. To the squat in *c*, with feet close together. By *d* the turn is made. A pose (*e*).

This simple turn is usually the first that beginners learn.

22a

22d

22e

## Single-Leg
## Kick Forward—Half Turn

**23.** Start is on the left leg with the right foot forward (*a*). In *b*, stepping to the left. These steps develop momentum. Weight is on the left foot in *c*. Ready to kick the right leg forward (*d*). The kick is straight toward the end of the beam. In *e*, a pivot on the left foot. The right leg swings forward in *f*.

23*a*

23*d*

23*e*

24*a*

24*b*

23b

23c

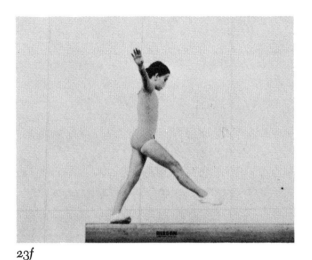

23f

## Single-Leg
## Kick Backward—Half Turn

**24.** Right leg is forward and ready to swing to the rear in *a*. As the right leg swings back in a straight line, there is a pivot on the left foot (*b*). The half turn has been completed in *c* and the right foot is forward. In *d*, a posed position.

24c

24d

# Half Squat, Half Straddle—
# Three-Quarter Turn

**25.** The start is in a half-squat, half-straddle
position (*a*). Arms are ready to swing. In *b*
both the right arm and the left leg have swung.
The left leg is moving toward the beam. By *c*
the left leg has swung around the right foot,
and a squat position has been reached. The
turn is continued with a pivot on both feet (*d*),
and is completed in *e*.

25*a*

25*d*

25*e*

25b

25c

A simple variation of this type of turn. As you advance, the turn can be made more elaborate.

## Tuck Jump—One Half Turn

**26.** A standing position in *a*. In *b*, a squat position in which the legs are coiled and the arms ready to swing. Legs are springing and arms swinging upward in *c*. By *d* the jump has been made. Legs are tucked. The turn is already underway. In *e* the half turn has been completed. The legs are extending for the landing, shown in *f*. The squat position (*g*).

26a

26b

26e

26c

26d

26f

26g

# Full Turn on One Leg

**27.** Stepping forward to the left foot (*a*). In *b* the arms are ready to supply momentum. Weight is shifting to the left leg in *c*, and the right leg is being brought upward. In *d* the right leg is bent. Turn is partially completed. The turn continues on one foot in *e*. By *f* the turn is about three-quarters complete. Finish of the turn and a lunge (*g*).

27*a*

27*b*

27*e*

27*f*

27c

27d

27g

As in most turns, many variations are possible. The turn can be carried out on either leg and in either direction. The free leg can assume different positions.

# Balances and Poses

**28.** Five suggested poses are seen in *a*. These poses have one thing in common. The girls are looking away from the beam instead of along it, which is the natural tendency. Variety in the direction of the face and vision adds attractiveness.

In *b*, a scat. The rear arm helps pull to a split. The body stays as high as possible while still maintaining balance. In *c*, a leg pull-up to the side. Again, one hand is used to get a split.

Photo *d* shows basically an arabesque with support of the hand on the knee. In *e*, a back arch over the end of the beam—a very pretty move, but it must be entered quickly and gracefully and left the same way.

In *f*, a shoulder rise position, in *g*, a swan position that can be done out of a forward or backward roll, and in *h*, a low-level pose in which vision is away from the beam.

A graceful leg lift (*i*). In *j*, a stag sit position

28b

28c

28g

28h

28i

with an imaginative arm treatment and in *k*, a recoil position that can offer contrast to a high leap.

Balances and poses are positions that are moved through. In general, held positions are discouraged. Many, many positions are possible, so only a relatively few can be shown as suggestions.

28a

28d

28e

28f

28j

28k

## V Seat to Knee Scale

**29.** A start in a Vseat balance, with arms to the side. In *b* the hands come down to the beam, the left leg is kept straight, and the right leg is beginning to bend. The hands have reached forward in *c*. The right leg is bent and tucked under the body. The left leg has swung back. In *d*, a knee scale position with the right arm raised.

*29a*

29b

29c

29d

The beginner usually does not have many
tumbling skills at her disposal. This sequence
shows how two poses or balances can be
linked together.

# Tuck Forward Roll

**30.** The start (*a*) is in a tuck position with the feet on the beam and the arms out to the side. In *b* the hands move to the English grip—thumbs together and hands down the sides of the beam. The legs extend so that the head can tuck under. To give confidence the spotter controls the direction in which the hips move. By *c* the head has tucked well under.

The roll continues in *d*. Legs are straight in a pike position. Elbows are squeezed in so that the arms can give effective control. Beginners often find it necessary to place the hands under the beam for greater control. This position of the hands does deduct fractions of a point but may be needed to keep from falling off the beam. In *e* the hips are being lowered to the beam. Effective use of the arms can help steer the hips to the beam. The roll is continued to a squat in *f*, and to the feet (*g*) for the completion of the skill.

30*a*

30*b*

30*e*

30c

30d

30f

30g

# Pike Forward Roll

**31.** An erect starting position with the arms overhead (*a*). In *b* the arms complete a circular motion as the upper body moves toward the beam. The circular movement of the arms is not an essential part of the skill, but it does add grace. The extension of the legs (*c*) will make it relatively easy to tuck the head. The arms take the weight of the body. In this way the upper body can be lowered smoothly so that the head does not bump the beam.

The head has been tucked in *d*. The arms are in control of the body. Legs are straight. From here on the action is just like that of the tuck forward roll. The roll continues in *e*. Body weight shifts to the feet (*f*). An erect position (*g*).

We have looked at two ways of starting a forward roll—the tuck and the pike positions. The forward roll can also be carried out from the scale and lunge positions.

31*a*

31*b*

31*e*

31*f*

31c

31d

31g

# Swedish Fall

**32.** Start (*a*) is from a scale position. Body
weight has fallen forward in *b*. Hands move
toward the beam to catch the weight. The body
remains basically in a straight-line position.
As the catch is made (*c*), the right leg comes
up hard and high. Both legs are straight.
The English grip is used. After *e*, there are many
options for the next move.

A pose in a front lying position (*f*). From
here it would be easy to straddle and sit up.

32*a*

32*d*

32*e*

33*a*

33*b*

32b

32c

32f

## Back Roll (Overhead)

**33.** The starting position (*a*) could be entered in various ways. An English grip is used, with the arms in a position to supply power. Legs are in a tight pike position. The roll is under way, and in *b* has continued so that the left foot is on the beam. The right leg is extended out to the side. The arms continue to push. By *c* the roll is almost completed.

From here there are many options. In this case (*d*) the right leg is brought forward.

33c

33d

## Back Shoulder Roll
## to Shoulder Stand

**34.** A lying position on the beam (*a*). Head is to one side of the beam. One hand is on its top and the other below. This position of the hands makes it possible to exert force. In *b* the legs are lifted to a pike position. The toes are driven upward toward the ceiling (*c*). In *d*, the shoulder stand position. This position is somewhat hard on the shoulder and can be uncomfortable. So when learning it, it's good to have a thick sweatshirt or some padding between the shoulder and the beam.

One of the ways of moving out of the shoulder stand appears in *e*. Various options exist for the move from *f*. For example, the gymnast can lie on the beam or straddle it.

34*a*

34*d*

34*e*

34*b*

34*c*

34*f*

# Kick Split— Lift and Straddle

**35.** Moving into a split from a kick position (*a*). The split starts in *b* and continues through *c* smoothly and quickly to *d*. The hands move down to the beam (*e*).

In *f*, a mixed grip with the hands on both sides of the beam. The arms lift the body here so that the legs are free to move. The legs are lifted off the beam and a rotation to the right is begun. By *g*, a half turn of the body is completed, and the gymnast sits on the beam in a straddle position. The legs are lifted to a V seat (*h*).

For the flexible girl splits are relatively easy. Splits are highly attractive on the beam, if carried out well. It's important to get into the split gracefully and quickly—and it's just as important to get out of it in an imaginative way.

35*c*

35*d*

35*g*

35*h*

35*a*

35*b*

35*e*

35*f*

## Some Other Ways
## to Get Out of the Split

**36.** Already in a split with the arms overhead (*a*). The right hand is brought down to the beam and placed underneath the leg in *b*. A push of the right arm will free the left leg. The trunk turns and the right foot is brought to the beam (*c*). There are then various options including movement to a stand.

36*a*

**37.** In the split (*a*). In *b* the right hand is on the beam to free the right leg. A push of the right hand and the bent right leg is placed on the beam (*c*). The gymnast sits on the side of the leg. With the weight sitting on the right leg the left leg is now free to permit an attractive pose (*d*).

37*c*

36b

36c

37a

37b

37d

# Headstand to Forward Roll

**38.** A standing position with the arms overhead (*a*). Movement forward and down toward the beam (*b*). Hands on the beam in the English grip (*c*). The arms are going to take the weight of the body. In *d*, because the weight is on the arms, the head can move gently to the beam. The head and hands make a tripod in *e*, though the tripod is somewhat limited by the width of the beam. It's important to have the head forward of the hands. The legs are being brought up straight.

The headstand position (*f*). A tuck position could be used, but the extended legs make the skill more attractive. The head is tucked under, and the body rolls forward in *g*. The roll continues (*h*). The head is being brought up. The right foot is placed on the beam (*i*). There is still momentum, which will help bring the gymnast to her feet in a standing position (*j*). The gymnast has started the roll in a standing position and finished in a standing position.

38c

38d

38g

38h

38a

38b

38e

38f

38i

38j

# No-Handed Forward Roll

**39.** Start is from a lunge (*a*). It could be made from a squat, but the lunge position is more attractive. In *b* arms are circling back and around, then (*c*) pointing straight down on each side of the beam. In this way the arms act as a guide. Later on, they can be to the sides. The left knee is well bent. Hips are high. The head will be well tucked in.

A full tuck of the head so that the roll is really on the upper back (d). The hands are clear of the beam and do not help. The spotter is ready to make the landing more gentle.
The roll is continued in *e*, with the head starting to lift, until *f* is reached without hesitation.
Feet on the beam (*g*) and to a standing position.

39*a*

39*b*

39*e*

39*f*

39c

39d

39g

39h

# Back Walkover

**40.** The gymnast stands straight and tall with the arms overhead (*a*). One foot is placed forward for balance. The spotter has her back to the gymnast so that she will be able to move along with her. At the same time, the spotter is in a better position to observe hand and foot placement. Movement starts with the head dropping back (*b*). The arms do not whip. In *c* the hands continue down toward the beam to an English grip. The right leg kicks upward. The hands land fairly close to the left leg, and this requires good flexibility. The short distance between the left foot and the hands makes it easier to get the hips over.

In *d*, passing through the handstand with the legs in a split position. The gymnast can see her foot descending in *e*. The right foot is placed on the beam (*f*). Moving upward (*g*) toward the stand to a standing position (*h*).

The back walkover should first be perfected on the floor before being used on the beam.

40*a*

40*b*

40*e*

40*f*

40c

40d

40g

40h

# Cartwheel

**41.** One leg forward, arms overhead (*a*).
In *b*, a normal hand position on the beam, with
fingers pointed toward the spotter. Through the
handstand position (*c*). A good wide straddle.
The spotter is ready to help with both hands.
The right leg lowers to the beam in *d*. Now
the basic job of the spotter is to make sure that
the foot reaches the beam. Foot is on the beam
in *e*. Beginning of extension. In *f*, a standing
position.

41*a*

41*d*

41*e*

41b

41c

41f

A cartwheel has to be performed on the beam with great precision. For this reason there should be preparation before the cartwheel is actually tried on the beam. It can be performed on the floor along a straight line and then on a low beam.

# Forward Tinsica

**42.** The start (*a*) is with one leg extended and arms overhead. As the gymnast moves forward and downward, one arm is lowered to prepare for an alternate hand placement (*b*). The alternate landing of the hands has been made in *c*. Through the handstand position, the spotter helps support and control. The quarter turn has been made in *d*. The right foot lands close to the hand to make it easier to come to a stand. To a stand (*e*) and a pose (*f*).

42a

42d

42e

42b

42c

42f

The tinsica has the features of both the cartwheel and the front walkover. It starts like a cartwheel, but there is a twist of the body that changes direction from sideways to forward.

# Valdez

**43.** As in floor exercise, the valdez starts
in a sitting position with one leg extended
forward (*a*). The other leg is drawn up close
to the hips. The left arm is straight down with
the thumb along the side of the beam. Fingers
are toward the spotter. The right arm is
forward.

Several important events happen at the same
time in *b*. The right arm drives backward.
The body arches. A powerful push from the
left leg. A vigorous kick of the right leg. In *c*,
the right hand is near the beam. Head is well
back. Right leg is kicking upward and back.
The left leg has finished its strong push
off the beam.

Close to a back-tinsica walkover position (*d*).
The right foot is placed on the beam (*e*). In
*f*, a standing position.

43*a*

43*d*

43*e*

43b

43c

43f

# English Handstand to Forward Roll

**44.** Starting from an erect position with arms overhead (*a*). In *b*, reaching forward to put the hands on the beam. The English grip is used. The gymnast has kicked up to a handstand in *c*. The legs are in a double stag. The double stag makes it easier to control balance. By *d* control has been established, and the legs extend.

With the arms gently lowering the body, the head reaches through the hands (*e*) so that the roll is made on the back of the head and the upper body. The hips come down to continue the roll (*f*). Movement toward the stand (*g*). In *h*, a pose.

44*a*

44*b*

44*e*

44*f*

44c

44d

44g

44h

# Handstand—Reverse Press

**45.** Start is erect with one leg forward (*a*). The approach to the handstand (*b*) is like that of the cartwheel. Handstand position is reached in *c*. (Earlier, when we were talking about mounts, we mentioned the handstand mount. This sequence shows a good way to get out of the handstand mount.) The legs are already moving apart to begin the straddle. The straddle (*d*) should be highly controlled. Hips lower and the legs rotate in *e*. As the legs lower (*f*), the shoulders move forward in front of the beam. The feet remain clear of the beam as they travel forward (*g*) to a straddle position (*h*).

45*a*

45*b*

45*e*

45*f*

45c

45d

45g

45h

## Jumping Dismounts

**46.** A standing position on the end of the beam (*a*). The legs bend and the arms swing in *b*. Both the extension of the legs and the swing of the arms create lift. A stag position in the air (*c*). The legs are extended and reaching toward the mat (*d*). Upon landing (*e*) the legs are only partially bent. A standing position with the arms over the head (*f*). In *g*, a stag position with a different arm position. A straddle position (*h*).

46*a*

46*d*

46*g*

46*h*

46b

46c

46e

46f

The jumping dismounts are usually the first
to be learned. They are relatively easy and give
the beginner a chance to learn some of the
basic principles of dismounting, such as a soft
landing and control. As the photos indicate, a
number of different positions can be taken in
the air.

# Knee Scale Dismount
# (with Hand Support)

**47.** The dismount is already underway in *a*.
The left leg has swung downward to begin a
pendulum-like movement. In *b* the left leg is
now swinging upward. The swing of the left
leg and a push from the right leg lift the legs in
the air (*c*). The legs are coming together and
descending in *d*. A soft landing. The right
hand is on the beam for balance (*e*). An erect
position with the arms overhead (*f*).

47*a*

47*d*

47*e*

47*b*

47*c*

47*f*

# Fence Dismount

**48.** A front support position (*a*). Arms are
on the beam with the English grip. Left toe
is curled under on the beam. Right leg is
extended high and back. In *b*, a pendulum
action of the right leg to build up momentum.
The legs are lifted (*c*) by the swing of the
right leg and a push from the left leg. The
legs are together as they descend (*d*). A soft
landing with support from the beam (*e*).
Erect position with the hands overhead (*f*).

48*a*

48*b*

48*e*

48c

48d

48f

# Roundoff
# (from End of Beam)

**49.** The weight is over the left foot with
the right foot pointed forward (*a*). Arms are
overhead. Hands are moving toward the beam
and weight has shifted to the right foot in *b*.
In *c*, moving up to the handstand position.
Legs together in readiness to push off (*d*).
A push-off of the arms and a snap down of the
legs (*e*). A quarter turn has been made so
that the gymnast is facing the beam. A soft
and controlled landing (*f*) and standing position
with the arms overhead (*g*).

49*a*

49*d*

49*e*

49*b*

49*c*

49*f*

49*g*

# Handstand Half-Turn Dismount

**50.** The start of movement to a handstand (*a*) and hands nearing the beam (*b*). In *c* legs are moving up. The handstand position (*d*). Here a critical point is that the gymnast should not be completely on balance. It's important that the center of body weight should be toward the spotter. Only in this way can there be a good dismount. By *e* the body weight has shifted to the left arm, and a twist of the trunk is made. The right hand is leaving the beam.

In *f* the legs are coming down next to the beam. The landing (*g*) and an erect position with the hands overhead (*h*).

50*a*

50*b*

50*e*

50*f*

50c

50d

50g

50h

# Handspring (off End)

**51.** Position for the handstand (*a*). Arms are overhead, and weight is over the left leg. The spotter is ready to assist. In *b*, nearing the handstand. The English grip is to be used. The spotter supports by grasping the upper left arm.

Up toward the handstand (*c*). The spotter places her right hand on the gymnast's back. The legs have gone by the head in *d*. The important action of the arms takes place. It is important that the arms push so there is a spring from the hands. This pushing action makes the skill both more attractive and safer.

Good height made possible by the push from the beam (*e*). The spotter is ready to help. In *f*, a reaching out of the legs; a critical part of the landing.

A partial bending of the knees for a controlled and soft landing (*g*). Extending to a stand (*h*).

51*a*

51*b*

51*e*

51*f*

51c

51d

51g

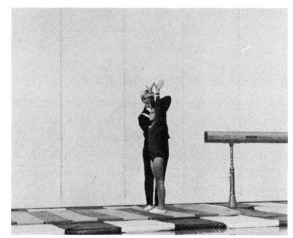

51h

# Baroni (with Spotting)

**52.** The baroni shown here starts from a stand (*a*). Later on, it can be carried out from a run. But in the early stages a standing start is easier for both the gymnast and the spotter. The spotter's position is at the end of the beam and slightly to one side or the other, depending on the leg used by the gymnast.

Weight shifts to the left foot in *b*. The spotter is ready. The gymnast is thinking of her experience in carrying out the roundoff.

Photo *c* is highly significant. The drop of the upper body and head has to be just right.

The head cannot remain at its original height. Yet it should not drop too much. The left leg is ready to drive, and the right leg is thrown vigorously upward. The legs create height. The spotter aids both height and control. The gymnast can see the mat and will be able to see it all the way through the skill.

The twist of the body is underway in *d* and completed in *e*. The legs snap down (*f*) and the upper body rises to an erect position, facing the beam (*g*).

52*a*

52*b*

52*e*

52*f*

52c

52d

52g

The baroni is a spectacular dismount that appears difficult. But good spotting and confidence can make the skill relatively easy to master. Before trying the baroni it is best that the roundoff be learned in floor exercise.

# Baroni (without Spotting)

**53.** After about a dozen or so spots, the skill can usually be carried out without spotting. Also, this dismount can be approached from a run. The baroni can be done off the middle of the balance beam, and it is even more spectacular when carried out in this way.

53*a*

53*b*

53*e*

53c

53d

53f

53g

# Back-Somie Dismount (off End of Beam)

**54.** The starting position is especially posed (*a*). Usually, this position is reached from some other skills such as a roundoff. Arms are in a stretch position. Spotter has his hand on the gymnast's back. In *b* the gymnast starts to sit back so as to be slightly off balance. The goals are to be clear of the beam and yet get great height.

Legs move toward a tuck position in *c* and head is starting back. In *d*, rotation of the body. Vision is now toward the mat. A soft controlled landing (*e*). Erect position (*f*).

The back-somie dismount can also be made from the center or any part of the beam. Before trying this skill from the beam it's a good idea to have some experience with the back somie from the floor.

54*a*

54*d*

54*e*

54*b*

54*c*

54*f*

# Front-Somie Dismount (off End of Beam)

**55.** A running approach (*a*). The take-off (*b*) is from both feet. One foot is slightly ahead of the other so that there can be a fuller contact with the beam. In *c* the upper body is lowering as the legs drive upward. There is a full effort to get good hip height—achieved in *d*. The legs and head are tucked to aid rotation of the body.

In *e*, starting to open from the tuck. In *f*, the legs are extending. Extension of the legs at this point slows down the rotation so that the gymnast won't land too far forward.

A soft and controlled landing (*g*)—always so important in the dismount.

The front-somie dismount can also be carried out from nearly every part of the beam. When done from the middle of the beam, the dismount is almost parallel to the beam. The body is thrown to one side so that the beam is cleared.

55*a*

55*b*

55*e*

55*f*

55c

55d

55g

55h

## Combination One

**56.** A balance position—steps—a turn on both feet—steps—a back walkover—lunge—pose.

56a

56d

56e

56h

56i

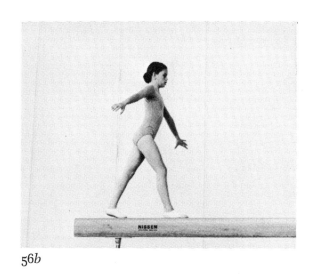

56b

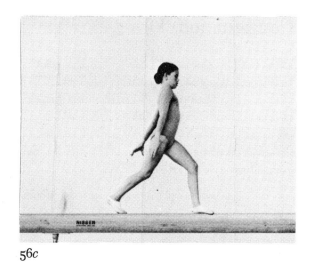

56c

56f

56g

56j

56k

## Combination Two

**57.** A short pose near the end of the beam (*a*). The left leg kicks forward (*b*). Toward a lunge (*c*). The lunge (*d*). No-handed forward roll (*e*). Continuing the roll (*f*). Squat position (*g*). Tuck jump (*h*). Landing with the position of the feet changed (*i*). Ready for a kick turn (*j*). A pose (*k*).

57*a*

57*d*

57*e*

57*h*

57*i*

57b

57c

57f

57g

57j

57k

# *Uneven Parallel Bars*

## ABOUT THE UNEVEN PARALLEL BARS

The development of the uneven parallel bars has been one of the happiest events in the history of sport. Probably the first "bar" was a tree limb. If we go back in imagination, even thousands of years ago, it's easy to picture youngsters exercising on almost any object that could have served as a bar. There must have been delight and achievement of hanging, swinging, turning, and supporting even then.

The bars have long been an important part of men's gymnastics. They have the horizontal bar and the parallel bars. These two pieces of gymnastic equipment place a premium on great physical strength.

When girls turned to gymnastics, they used the parallel bars of the men. Often the bars were lowered a bit. The lowering of the bars did not make that much of a difference—the significant difference was yet to come.

Somwhere along the way someone came up with the idea that the event could be made better for girls if the bars were of different heights. It may not have been only one person who thought of this idea; perhaps a number of people talked it over. In any case, during the 1930s the uneven parallel bars began to appear in competition. They took hold. They showed up in the 1936 Olympic Games. The uneven parallel bars became established at the 1952 Olympic Games. Since that time the event has been competed all over the world and is now standard in all competitions.

*Value.* Of course, the great value was the setting for an activity that provided almost all that athletics can offer—the spectacular, the sense of achievement, the healthful habits that extend through life. But in addition a way of confronting appropriate sports activity was made available for girls. Maybe you'll disagree, but it doesn't seem to work out too well when masculine sports are precisely imitated by girls. It seems best that there be a variation that can make the activity more appropriate for girls.

The uneven parallel bars make for a very special event. A showcase is provided for girls' gymnastics at its finest. Movements requiring great strength are not needed, and even discouraged. Instead, the premium is on swinging and circling. Millions of girls all over the world at all ages and all levels of ability are gaining great personal benefits from the uneven bars—all the way from the national performer who is seen on television to the youngster in the physical-education class.

*Dimensions.* The heights of the bars are specified in the metric system and work out as follows. The high bar or upper bar is about 7 feet 6 inches. The height of the low bar is about 5 feet. The distance between the uprights that support the bars is about 1½ feet. This latter distance can be adjusted to take account of the gymnast's height. These are the dimensions now. But the international federation responsible for the rules may change the measurements or even give the competitors options concerning bar heights.

The resiliency or "flex" of the bars is one of their important features. This "flex" produces a number of effects. It affects timing. It makes body contact with the bar gentler. And it creates a bounce effect that increases momentum.

# OUR APPROACH

As you read and look at the photo sequences, you will see the approach that we are taking to learning the skills. In general, anyone who wants to teach anything does have the problem of deciding upon the best order or sequence in which things should be learned. This is always hard to know. There are two guidelines, and though both are useful, neither is sure-fire. However, it does seem reasonable that one skill should be built upon another. For example, it works out best to take beginning French before trying intermediate French. The related guideline, that of progressive difficulty, surely seems at first glance a good one. Yet it's still hard to tell. What might be a difficult skill for one person could be an easy one for somebody else.

We've tried to combine a number of approaches in hopes of coming up with what will be most useful to you.

We do know that in any performance a number of things have to happen. There has got to be a mount to the bar followed by a number of skills, including kips, circles, and other skills—and then, of course, a dismount. Each can be considered a section of a full routine. So we will approach each section separately. Within each section we'll try to build skill on skill. We'll try to start with the skills that seem most simple and then go on to others that appear more complex. But you, of course, will remember that skills should be mastered well. They are not just stepping-stones to more sophisticated activity. In themselves they are important. Even when you go very far, you will want to carry out the simpler skills well.

When you compare the various sports events, it does seem that the gymnast is called upon to learn more skills than any other athlete. That is surely true. But on the other hand the great variety of gymnastic skills does not have to be all that bewildering. There are things you learn to do that carry over from one skill to the next. You will see these patterns emerge. As an example, look for the jump and glide when we are talking about kips. When this skill is learned, it provides a base for carrying out many other skills.

Single skills are put together to form appropriate combinations. A skill has to blend into the next one. A smooth performance then means knowing the skills that best go together. So we ought to spend some time on combinations. Then the combinations can be further put together to form a full routine.

# SAFETY

*Equipment.* Safety starts with good equipment. That should not be too great a problem, since excellent and reliable equipment is made by the various companies. Even the finest equipment should be checked before each practice session. Though the instructor assumes primary responsibility for the equipment, it is a good idea for you to work with him or her. In this way you become familiar with the equipment and acquire the habit of checking it out.

Mats are placed under the bars and extend lengthwise far enough to provide a safe landing for any dismount. Mats, although next to each other, should never overlap. Overlapping mats make for a bulge or bump that could twist an ankle. An ideal mat arrangement would be one in which the mats are tailored to surround the uprights holding the bars.

Gymnastic chalk should always be on hand to reduce the chances of the hands slipping off the bar.

*Spotting.* This has two important purposes—safety and learning. The trained spotter can prevent many falls. Spotting is such a vital part of gymnastics that every gymnast should learn to be good at it. The ability to spot helps in two ways. First, by understanding spotting you can take better advantage of the spotting that others do for you. Second, of course, you can be of great help to your teammates.

Many skills can be practiced on either the low bar or the high bar. It is best to use the low bar, because the spotting can be much more effective. The girls of average height will have trouble spotting a teammate on the high bar.

We will throughout the book be paying a great deal of attention to spotting. In nearly ever photo sequence you will be seeing the work of the spotter, and we will also be talking about the spotting. We hope you will get a clear idea of how spotting is used for both safety and learning. It should be mentioned that the spotter has to pay some attention to her own safety. She is in no great danger, but it's best to avoid bruises. Then too, there are certain fundamentals for the spotter to learn. For example, you will see that she keeps her arms under, not over, the bars. The idea is not to get your arms between the bar and the weight of the performer. Also, it's important to know where the flying feet of the gymnast are likely to go so that you can avoid them.

*Getting good.* The ability to master a skill may be the best safeguard of all. When you are good at what you are doing, danger decreases. There has to be a nice balance between perfecting simpler skills and going on to new ones. The gymnast keeps an adventuresome attitude but still pays attention to safety.

# WARMING UP

Warming up is so important that it has to be talked about in all sections of a book on gymnastics. The importance of the warm-up is seldom realized right away. It seems to take experience. The beginner tries to avoid the warm-up; the expert always warms up thoroughly. In most sports activities the goal of the warm-up is to get the blood circulating and to make the muscles more supple. The warm-up for gymnastics does all of this—and much more.

The basic warm-up usually takes place on the floor and includes tumbling exercises. This is true no matter what the event to be practiced. Often the basic warm-up is carried out anyway before the gymnast turns to the uneven parallel bars. If so, then the gymnast can give attention to the exercises that really go beyond the basic warm-up. She then carries out the exercises that relate to performance on the uneven parallel bars. The appropriate muscles become more flexible and stronger.

# Inverted-Tuck
# Knee-Rise Mount

A good starting point for learning mounts.
It's an easy and safe way to get up on the bars.

**1.** A standing position with the hands on the bar (*a*). A jump to an inverted-tuck position (*b*). Hips are high. It's good training to learn to hold this position. In *c* one leg is being tucked through to hook the leg over the bar. The other leg is extended in *d*. Arms are kept straight. The extended leg has been swung downward in *e*, making for a lever action that lifts the upper body. In *f*, a stride position on the bar with the hands in a regular grip.

Spotting: The important spotting is shown in *d* and *e*, where the spotter helps drive the extended leg downward to help the upper body rise.

1*a*

1*d*

1*e*

1b

1c

1f

# Back Hip-Circle Mount

**2.** Standing with a regular grip on the bar (*a*). A step forward (*b*). Readiness to kick (*c*). The right leg is kicked forward in *d*. Arms are bent and the chin comes toward the bar. Hips are coming toward and over the bar (*e*). The circular movement continues in *f* with the hips reaching the bar. Body is parallel to the floor in *g*. Arms are still bent. The arms have extended in *h*. The gymnast is in a front support.

What happens in the first three photos is important. The gymnast thinks, "Step, kick, and chin."

Spotting: In *e* the spotter helps lift the hips. The spotter also helps maintain the parallel body position (*g*).

2a

2b

2e

2f

2c

2d

2g

2h

# Whip Pike Mount

A good mount for beginners. The upper bar may be a bit high for most youngsters to reach directly, but in most competitions lifting assistance is allowed.

**3.** The hang from the upper bar (*a*). The legs are lifted sharply (*b*). There is no full body swing. The legs are lifted from the hips. The legs are thrust backward (*c*) so that the body is hyperextended. In *d*, a pike in which the legs shoot upward. Extension of the legs over the low bar (*e*). The body is straight.

Spotting: The spotter helps in keeping the whole body from swinging.

3*a*

3*c*

# Vaulting Back Hip-Circle Mount

**4.** A running approach to the reuther board (*a*) In *b* the board is hit with both feet. The bar is grasped. A thrust up to a front support (*c*). It is a free front support in that the hips are not resting on the bar. The upper body is kept high (*d*) as the hips move into the bar. When the hips contact the bar (*e*), the

shoulders drop back. The backward circular action continues in *f* and *g*. In *h*, a front support.

Spotting: In *c* and *d* the spotter makes sure that the hips make contact with the bar.

4a

4b

4e

4f

4c

4d

4g

4h

## Squat Vault Mounts

**5.** The running approach has been made (*a*). The lift from the board. Hands on the bar (*b*). The legs begin to swing to the right. It could be to the left, depending on the preferred side. As the legs swing to the right (*c*), the right hand has to be removed from the bar to allow the legs to pass. This means that body weight has to be centered over the left arm. The legs have passed over the bar in *d*, so the right arm can now return to the bar. In *e*, a rear sitting position on the low bar. Sometimes a beginner finds it best to put her hand on the upper bar to steady herself.

Spotting: The spotter has to know what the gymnast intends to do. The spotter is away from the direction in which the gymnast is going to swing her legs.

5*c*

5*d*

6*a*

6*b*

5a

5b

5e

**6.** The run brings the gymnast to a take-off from two feet (*a*). It's important that the lift from the board be high and straight up. Arm action helps the lift of the body. Hip height is vital (*b*). Both the drive off the board and arm action get the hips high enough to carry out the mount. Hip height allows the legs to be tucked through. In *c* the feet land on the lower bar. A grasp of the upper bar offers support (*d*).

6c

6d

# Front Hip-Circle Vault Mount

**7.** A running approach (*a*). Proper use of the board can greatly increase lift and let you rise almost straight up. A take-off from both feet (*b*). Arms are extended overhead. In *c*, still rising. The hips will go above the bar. A full extended position is held. There is still no contact with the bar.

Hips are above the bar in *d* and now the thighs make contact with the bar. Body is still extended. A pike position, and rotation begins (*e*). The arms whip. The bar is grasped (*f*), and rotation continues (*g*) to a front support.

It's important to start with a straight body and then quickly pike at the right time so that you will rotate around the bar.

Spotting: The spotter tries to keep the performer's hips close to the bar.

7a

7b

7e

7f

7c

7d

7g

7h

## Straddle over Vault Mount

**8.** A running approach with take-off off the board from both feet. The arms reach for the lower bar (*a*). Power is needed. Both the drive off the board and the arms have to supply lift. In *b* power has supplied a high and straight-up lift, and the legs are starting to straddle. The legs are straddled and over the bar by *c*. The hands are pushing off the bar to supply extra lift. In *d*, as the legs start to come together, the hands reach to the upper bar. Arms have grasped the upper bar (*e*). This is a piked sitting position on the low bar—a good position from which to continue a routine.

Spotting: The spotters are in standby positions ready to break any fall that might occur.

8*a*

8*d*

*8b*

*8c*

*8e*

# Straddle over to Long Hand on High Bar—Vault Mount

This mount is really an extension of the straddle over vault mount that we've just been looking at. Instead of ending sitting on the lower bar you continue to a long hand on the high bar. Actually, the mount to the high bar completes the basic task. But you can't be left hanging there, so further photos are included. A kip to the upper bar is a good option.

**9.** A good take-off from the board is needed, because body height (*a*) is important. Body height is increased by the push of the arms from the lower bar. By *b* fine body height has resulted from the take-off and arm action. The legs have cleared the lower bar, and the arms are starting to reach for the upper bar. In *c* the arms near the upper bar and the legs lower. The high bar is grasped in *d*. The legs are

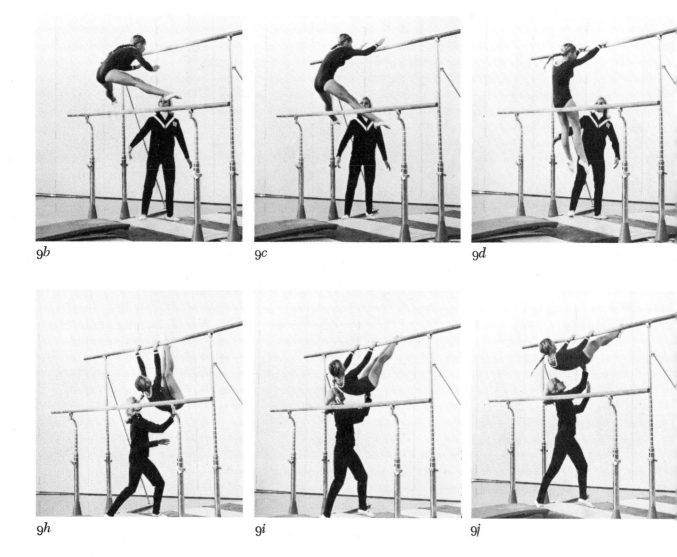

9*b*　　　　9*c*　　　　9*d*

9*h*　　　　9*i*　　　　9*j*

coming together. In *e* the body is extending.

Extension to a position past the upper bar appears in *f*. Various options exist at this point. Here, the gymnast is getting ready to kip to the upper bar. In *g*, piking—ready for the kip. Ankles go to the upper bar (*h*). Hips are out past the upper bar. In *i* kip action starts. Kip action continues (*j, k, l, m*) to a front support on the upper bar.

9*a*

*e*  9*f*  9*g*

9*l*  9*m*

# Learning Progression for Glide Kip—Jump and Glide

The teacher or spotter can help the gymnast get a feel for the jump and glide. In this learning progression there is no jump for the bar.

**10.** The teacher holds the hips in the back position (*a*). The gymnast now has a good chance to visualize the straight line running from the hips to the hands. In *b* knees are bent just to relieve tension during the learning process. As the jump is made (*c*), the teacher pulls back the hips to emphasize correct position. Upper body remains in alignment.

Glide starts in *d* and continues in *e* to full extension of the body (*f*).

10*a*

10*c*

10*d*

10*b*

10*e*

10*f*

# Learning Progression for Glide Kip—Kip Action

In the photo series before this we looked at the learning process up to the glide. Now we can concentrate on the kip.

**11.** The teacher supports the extended body position that comes at the end of the glide (*a*). A very fast pike is emphasized (*b*). When the ankles go by the lower bar, the hips should still be in front of the lower bar. Quickness of the upward movement of the legs is vital. The next actions can be learned on the mat. The position shown in (*b*) is actually transferred to the mat in *c*. Arm action and leg action are simulated in *d* and *e*. The important idea is to think of the legs shooting straight up.

11*a*

11*d*

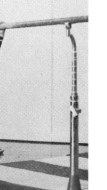

11b

11c

11e

## Glide Kip to Front Support

The kip is one of the most important of all gymnastic skills. It is not easily learned. It requires strength, coordination, and timing. Even so, work on the kip starts early in the gymnast's career. In brief, get introduced to the kip right away but don't worry about not mastering it right away.

**12.** A position is taken back of the bar (*a*). You stand as far back as you can while still being able to jump to the bar with comfort. Knees are bent (*b*). Start of the jump. Photo *c* shows a key moment. Head remains low. Hips are back—not up. There is a straight line from the hands to the hips. The feet remain fairly close to the floor. The pike is not sharp.

12a

12b

12f

12g

12h

In *d*, a swinging out under the bar. The feet are just clear of the mat; arms are extended. In *e*, an extended body position in front of the bar. The more extension the better, but the amount of extension depends on body strength. At this point, the glide has been made.

The body pikes in *f*. Ankles start toward the bar. As the ankles pass by the bar (*g*), the hips are still rising. It is important to shoot the legs before the hips drop. In *h*, think of your feet going to the ceiling. Think of pulling the bar to your hips. The arms have been pushing down on the bar in *i*. Legs thrust down. Front support (*j*).

c

12d

12e

i

12j

## Glide Kip—Single-Leg Shoot-Through Mount

We've just been emphasizing the jump and glide. This important skill is now used again. The first part of this mount is like the previous one. Mastering the jump and glide prepares you for a series of mounts. It also get you ready to carry out various skills on the bars.

**13.** Ready for the jump (*a*). The jump begins (*b*). Hands near the bar (*c*). Hips are back. In *d* spotter emphasizes the back position of the hips. Glide (*e*) and extension (*f*).

The legs shoot upward in *g*. The left leg leads so that it will be ready to shoot between the arms. The hips are still forward and moving upward. In *h* the left foot is between the hands. Hips are still out in front of the bar. In *i* the arms remain straight as they exert pressure on the bar. Left leg is straight and pointing toward the ceiling. A stride position (*j*).

13*a*

13*d*

13*g*

13*h*

13b

13c

13e

13f

13i

13j

## Glide-Kip Catch Mount

Again, the basic skills of jump and glide supply the base for the mount.

**14.** The jump has been made in *a*. Hips are well back. In *b*, glide toward extension of the body. A fast pike with the legs shooting straight up (*c*). Hips are rising in *d*. It's important that they continue to rise before attention is turned to the upper bar. In *e*, hips are high. Body is extended. Arms are exerting pressure to lift the upper body.

A reach for the high bar (*f*) and upper bar is grasped (*g*). A long hang.

14*a*

14*d*

14*g*

14b

14c

14e

14f

14h

# Double-Leg Rise
# to High Bar

One of the most basic and simple ways to get from the lower bar to the upper bar.

**15.** Hands on the upper bar, feet on the lower bar (*a*). The body is in pike position. In *b* the shoulders relax and stretch to drop the hips. Downward pressure of the arms lifts the body (*c*). The arms remain straight. In *d* arms bend to exert more power. The feet push off the lower bar. This brings the upper body up and around the upper bar.

Feet have pushed off the lower bar in *e*. The action of the leg push and arm has made the upper body high and rotating. In *f*, extension to a front support.

15*a*

15*d*

15b

15c

15e

15f

## Stem Rise

Even though only one leg is involved, the basic concepts of the kip apply.

**16.**  Start is with one foot on the lower bar. The other leg is extended. In *b* the extended leg is brought up to and past the high bar. The idea is to get over the high bar, so the hips are forward of the high bar. The lead leg shoots directly upward in *c*. The left leg is beginning to drive off the low bar. Arm action adds to height. In *d*, shoulders are rising high above the upper bar. The arms are extended (*e*). A front support.

16*a*

16*d*

16*b*

16*c*

16*e*

# Kip from Low Bar to High Bar

**17.** A rear lying position with the hands on the high bar (*a*). Legs have been driven downward in *b*. The body is now more than extended. Compare with glide kip. The position is really similar to that achieved by the glide. In *c*, a fast pike. Legs shoot straight up (*d*). The legs continue to shoot straight up while the arms exert downward pressure on the upper bar (*e*).

Hips are to the upper bar in *f*. Shoulders are rising. Legs are extended forward. As the upper body continues upward and forward, the heels are kicked down and back (*g*). Legs remain straight.

Front support on the high bar (*h*).

17a

17d

17g

17b

17c

17e

17f

17h

# Kip from Long Hang

We have previously seen this kip from a mount.
It's easier to learn when you can start on
the bars.

**18.** Sitting on the low bar with the hands
on the high bar (*a*). Compare this position
to that of the jump before the glide used in a
mount. Legs and hips drive forward in *b*.
The forward position of the hips is important.
The kip, which should be becoming familiar to
you, appears in *c*. While the hips are forward
and rising, the ankles shoot straight upward.

   Ankles are going by the high bar in *d*. They
continue to rise. In *e*, legs thrust down and
back. The shoulders move upward and forward.
Upper body is above the bar by *f*. To a front
support (*g* and *h*).

18*a*

18*c*

18*f*

18b

18d

18e

18g

18h

# Front Stride Circle
# (or Front Mill Circle)

**19.** A stride position off the bar. Hands support the weight. A reverse grip is used. The first part of the circle is going to be done around the back leg. In *b*, starting to fall forward. The upper body remains straight. The lead leg stays extended. The gymnast thinks of stretching the leg forward.

The stretch position is maintained for the whole circle (*c*, *d*, *e*, and *f*). This is the crux of the skill.

A return to the starting position (*g* and *h*).

Spotting: The spotter stands behind the bar to help the gymnast complete the circle. The spotter never reaches over the bar. The spotter's right arm is under the bar and supporting the wrist as the circle starts. The spotter's left arm is ready to help complete the circle.

19*a*

19*c*

19*e*

19*f*

19*b*

19*d*

19*g*

19*h*

# Front Mill Catch

We've just looked at the front stride circle, or front mill circle. The first part of the front mill catch is exactly the same.

**20.** Stride position on the lower bar (*a*). Hips have been lifted off the bar and the circle starts (*b*). Lead leg is extended in *c*, with upper body straight. Straight body position is maintained in *d*. Hips are close to the low bar (*e*). The gymnast stays extended. In *f*, hands are moving toward the upper bar. The high bar is grasped in *g*, and the move is completed (*h*).

Spotting: The spotter's main task appears in *e*. The job is to help the gymnast reach the upper bar. The spotter must protect himself by keeping his head out of the way of flying feet.

20a

20d

20g

20b

20c

20e

20f

20h

## Back Hip Circle

We've already looked at a back hip-circle mount.

**21.** Front support position on the low bar with normal grip (*a*). In *b* legs are swung forward to get thrust.

The cast (*c*). Legs have swung back and parallel to the floor. Arms are straight. Shoulders are high. In *d* the low bar is hit in an extended position. Contact with the bar drives the legs forward and upward (*e*). Shoulders drop back.

Rotation around the bar (*f*). The upper body is raised (*g*). Front support (*h*).

21*a*

21*d*

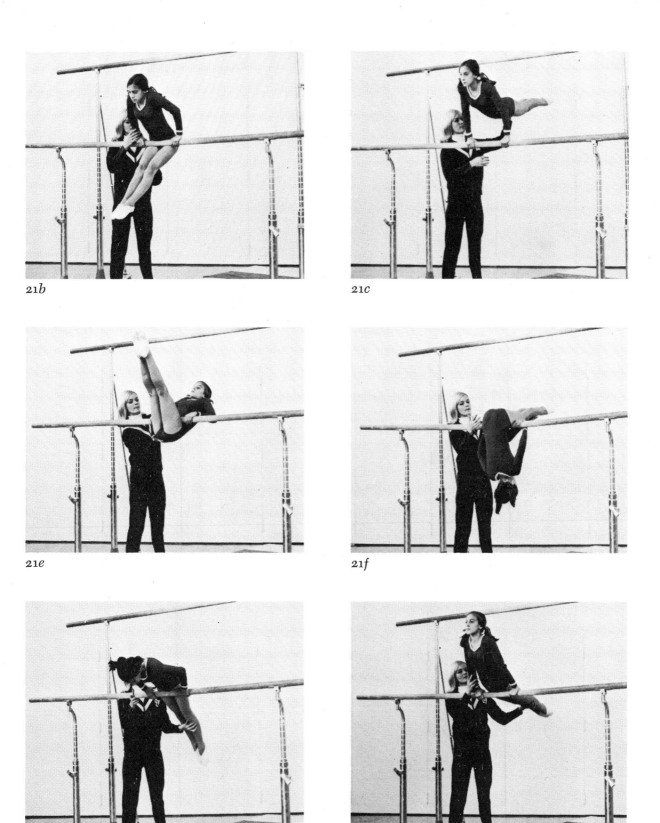

21b

21c

21e

21f

21g

21h

# Front Hip Circle

**22.** A front support but a very high one with the arms fully extended (*a*). The forward fall starts in a fully extended position (*b*). As the upper body falls, the legs rise. In *c*, a hard pike in which "the nose chases the knees." Rotation continues in *d*, and by *e* the circle is almost completed and the arms are ready to raise the upper body.

Cast and readiness for the next skill (*f*).

22*a*

22*b*

22c

22d

22e

22f

## Hip Pull over High Bar

**23.** Sitting on the low bar with the hands grasping the high bar. One leg is extended and the other is prepared to drive from the bar. In *b*, starting to chin. Extension of the lead leg (*c*). The other leg starts to push off the bar. In *d*, hips coming to the high bar. Head begins to lift (*e*).

Rotation around the upper bar (*f*). In *g*, body extending.

Front support on the upper bar (*h*).

23*a*

23*d*

23b

23c

23e

23f

23g

23h

# Jump to Back Hip Circle on High Bar

A good connecting move for intermediates.

**24.** Standing position on the lower bar (*a*). Balls of the feet are in contact. Hands grasp the upper bar. In *b*, lift comes from both the arms and the legs. The bend of the lower bar reflects leg drive.

Legs are lifting in *c*. Arms are straight.

Shoulders are over the bar. In *d*, a high-cast free support position. Elbows are straight. Shoulders are high (look back to the back hip-circle mount). Legs descend in *e* to develop momentum.

Hips contact the bar (*f*). Rotation (*g*) continues (*h*).

Front support on the high bar (*i*).

24*c*

24*f*

24*g*

24a

24b

24d

24e

24h

24i

## Knee-Hang Hip Circle

An excellent lead-up to other skills.

**25.** Sitting on the lower bar with hands on the upper bar (*a*). This position becomes more and more familiar. It's like the one that comes from the glide. In *b*, legs have moved up fast to an inverted-tuck position.

A hang from the knees with both arms extended (*c*). In *d* the lower bar is grasped. Arms are straight. Shoulders are forward of the bar.

The legs begin to extend in *e*. Keeping full body extension is important to the skill (*f*). The body makes contact with the bar (*g*). Extension is maintained all the way.

The quick pike is forced by the bar (*h*). There is no pike before reaching the bar. Rotation around the bar (*i*).

To a front support (*j*).

Spotting: Right arm of spotter helps shoulders to go forward. Left arm of spotter is used to insure hip height of gymnast.

25*a*

25*d*

25*g*

25*h*

25b

25c

25e

25f

25i

25j

# Front Seat Circle

**26.** Sitting on the lower bar ( *a* ). In *b* and *c* hips are lifted high and well back. The body pikes. The circle starts ( *d* ). Pike position is maintained. Circle continues in *e*. Pike position is kept. Legs are straight. With the circle almost completed ( *f* ) the straight legs are forced downward to raise the upper body.

Body is extended ( *g* ). In *h*, a sitting position. The circle has been completed.

26a

26d

26g

26b

26c

26e

26f

26h

Spotting: The spotter uses his right arm to steady the grip. Notice that the right arm is *under* the bar. The spotter's right arm is in position to help complete the circle.

# Hook Swing, Half Turn, Catch High Bar

**27.** Rear sitting position facing high bar (*a*). Regular grip. Hips are pulled backward so that the bar slides to the knees (*b*). Knees are bent forcefully to lock the bar (*c*). Upper body is still erect and high. Arms swing straight up and high to generate momentum (*d*). Hands have released the bar. In *e* hips are beginning to extend. The big circle of the arms continues. In *f*, a complete extension of the body from the knees.

The knees are the pivot point for the circle in *g*. Momentum developed earlier is being used. In *h* and *i* rotation is being completed and attention is turned to the high bar. The half turn is being made in *j* and *k*. Hands reach for the high bar. In *l*, a long hang from the high

27a  27b  27c

27g  27h  27i

bar. The half turn has put the gymnast in a good position to go on to another skill.

Spotting: The early job of the spotter is to make sure that the bar is locked at the knees. By g the spotter has two jobs—to keep the knees locked and to help with momentum if needed.

27d

27e

27f

27j

27k

27l

# Pike Sole Circle Forward—Regrasp High Bar

**28.** A squat position with the arches of the feet firmly against the lower bar. (*a*). A reverse grip. Legs extend in *b*. The main task is to keep the feet pressed solidly against the bar. The circle starts in *c*. The pull of the arms and the press of the legs keep the feet glued to the bar. The pike is so extreme that it is useful to think of "compressing" the body.

Compressed position is maintained. Soles of the feet are firm against the bar. In *e*, feet still in contact with the bar. In *f*, hips are about even with the bar. The feet come off the bar.

A reach to the high bar (*g*). In *h*, the long hang from the high bar.

Spotting: The spotter tries to keep the hands from slipping. Also, the spotter helps to keep the feet in contact with the bar. The final job of the spotter is to help the gymnast reach the upper bar.

28a

28b

28e

28f

28c

28d

28g

28h

# Straddle Sole Circle Underswing—Catch High Bar, Half Turn

**29.** Straddle position on the lower bar with legs extended (*a*). Regular grip. (This position can be reached in various ways.) The fingers curl very far under the bar. The pike is extreme . . . the chest is compressed to the legs. In *b*, falling into the circle. Important are the extreme pike or compression and the push of the legs against the bar and the pull of the arms.

The circle starts in *c*. Gravity does the work.

The gymnast keeps the tight pike and pressure against the bar. In *d*, the hips are starting to rise. The feet are kept on the bar. Hips rise as high as possible, and continue to rise in *e*. The hands are releasing. Legs are extending. In *f*, a half turn and a grasp of the high bar. Photo *g* shows good position for the next move—especially a wrap.

29*a*

29*d*

29*e*

*29b*

*29c*

*29f*

*29g*

# Straddle Sole Circle Forward To Glide Kip

**30.** A stand in the straddle position on the low bar with a hand on the high bar to help balance (*a*). Reaching down to grasp the bar (*b*). (This position could be reached in other ways. But in learning this is a good place to start.) The straddle position is kept in *c*. Legs are straight. A reverse grip on the bar. A tight pike position. Soles of the feet pressed against the bar. In *d* and *e*, circling the bar. Body remains compressed. The push of the legs and pull of the arms keep the soles of the feet firmly against the bar.

The hips are even with the bar (*f*). Still the reverse grip. In *g* the hips have moved higher. Hands have changed to a regular grip. In *h* the straddle guide is underway.

30*a*

30*b*

30*c*

30*g*

30*h*

30*i*

The now familiar kip action from the glide
(*i*, *j*, and *k*). In *l*, front support.

Spotting: Directed toward keeping the feet
against the bar and later toward supporting the
completion of the circle.

30e

30f

30k

30l

# Learning to Cast

It is a good idea to perfect the cast on the low bar. In this way the spotter can give more help.

**31.** Starting in a front support (*a*). Legs are swung downward (*b*). Legs are swung back (*c*). Hips are coming off the bar. Elbows remain straight. Legs move back (*d*). Body is extended, arms are straight. In *e*, a push away from the bar. Control is in the shoulders.

31*a*

31*b*

31c

31d

31e

Body is in alignment and parallel to the floor. The spotter supports the gymnast so that she can get a good feel for correct position.

# Lead-Up to Cast Wrap

In the previous photo sequence you saw the whole movement that began from the bar. In learning, the wrap can be more isolated.

**32.** One foot is against the low bar to supply a push backward (*a*). In *b*, kicking backward.

The spotter helps the gymnast swing well back of the upper bar (*c*). Photo *d* shows swing toward the bar. Straight body is emphasized.

In *e*, contact with the bar. Body remains straight. Start of the pike (*f*). Legs come up higher (*g*). Upper bar is released (*h*). In *i*, the circle continues. Front support (*j*).

32*c*

32*d*

32*g*

32*h*

32a

32b

32e

32f

32i

32j

## Cast-Wrap Hip Circle

**33.** Facing the lower bar from a front-support position on the upper bar (*a*). Legs swing downward and forward (*b*). In *c*, a cast backward. Elbows are straight. Legs are almost parallel to the floor. Shoulders are above the bar. Hips are clear of the bar.

In *d* the entire body is moved back. Arms are straight. Body is extended. Extension is controlled, with control in the shoulders. Body remains extended in *e* and *f*, where it makes contact with the lower bar.

It is important that the impact of the bar force the pike (*g*). In *h*, body is circling the bar at the hips. Hands let go. During the circling (*i*), hands are placed on the bar. In *j*, a front support.

Spotting: There is help with hip height (*d*) and slowing down the swing (*e*). The spotter makes sure the hips are in good contact with the bar (*g*).

33*c*

33*d*

33*g*

33*h*

33a

33b

33e

33f

33i

33j

# Underswing, Half-Turn Wrap from Rear Seat

**34.** Pike sit position on the low bar (a). Hands in a crossed mixed grip. This grip will help the half turn that is to come. In *b*, legs drive downward. Next, ankles are pulled up toward the high bar and elbows start to bend (*c*). As the ankles go by the high bar they shoot out to raise the hips (*d*).

Legs shoot outward in *e*. The turn starts. In *f*, gravity is bringing the legs downward. Turn is almost completed. In *g* contact with the bar has been made, and the pike has started.

The wrap (*h*) and front support (*i*).

An early drill to get ready to carry out an eagle. Both timing and orientation can be gotten before the full eagle.

34*c*

34*d*

34*g*

34*h*

34a

34b

34e

34f

34i

## Preparation for Eagle

**35.** Lying over the bar in a pike position (*a*). The legs swing back and forth. The whole body swings. On the second swing the gymnast is asked to "pop" (*b*). The hips are driven against the bar to make use of the bounce. Arms come up straight. The body arches. Heels kick backward. In *c*, a catch of the bar in an eagle grip. Feet are behind—not underneath. The eagle grip itself takes special attention and practice.

35*a*

35*b*

35*c*

## Cast-Wrap Eagle

**36.** Cast (*a*). In *b*, body is extended during the swing. Nearing the bar with the body still extended (*c*). In *d* pike is forced by contact with the bar.

Hands are free (*e*). Pressure of the hips keeps the gymnast in contact with the bar. In *f*, almost ready to "pop." The "pop" will come when the legs near the floor. (Look again at previous photo sequence.)

Arms upward in *g*. Body arched. An eagle grip on the bar (*h*). Legs are back.

36a

36d

36g

36b

36c

36e

36f

36h

Spotting: In *f* the spotter is ready to keep the "pop" from coming too soon. In *g* the spotting makes sure the legs continue backward.

## Single-Leg Shoot-Through

This is a good way to get from a front support
to a position in which a front mill circle can
be carried out. A basic move but not an easy one.

**37.** A front support (*a*). In *b*, legs are
swung forward to develop momentum. A cast
brings the hips off the bar (*c*). Hips are still
rising. Shoulders are forward in *d*. Hips are
high. Leg tucks through between the arms.

Weight is completely over the hands as the
leg extends through (*e*). In *f*, a stride position.
Weight is still supported by the hands.

37*a*

37*d*

37*b*

37*c*

37*e*

37*f*

# Double-Leg Shoot-Through

A move to make the transition from a front support to a seat position.

**38.** A front support ( *a* ). Legs pump or swing forward ( *b* ). In *c*, a cast that brings the hips off the bar. All the body weight is taken by the arms. Shoulders are well above the bar.

Hips are high in *d*, with good control. The start of a tight tuck. In *e* a very tight tuck as the legs are ready to come through between the arms.

The legs are extended through between the arms in *f*. Control is important. Movement is slowed down. There is a leaning back on the shoulders. In *g*, legs are extended.

*38a*

*38d*

*38e*

38b

38c

38f

38g

## Skin the Cat to Stride Support

A good move that permits the beginner and the intermediate to make use of both bars. The action can be carried out in a number of ways, and this is just one of them. Along the way there are many options.

**39.** Sitting on the low bar in a tight pike with the hands on the high bar (*a*). Arms fully extended (*b*). Body is hyperextended. In *c*, as the legs are pulled up they are helped by the rebounding of the bar.

An inverted-tuck position (*d*). Hips keep coming through. Ankles are going by the low bar in *e*. Legs are extended, and there is a slide down the bar (*f*).

An arch and an extension of the body. Head is up (*g*). Release of one hand (*h*).

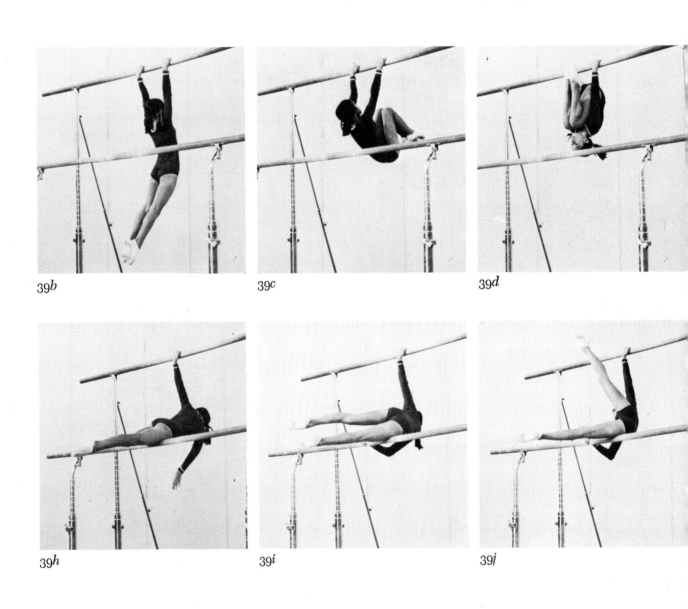

39*b*    39*c*    39*d*

39*h*    39*i*    39*j*

Extension of the body is important. In *i*, a rollover on one thigh. The right hand goes to the low bar. The left leg is ready to scissor and kick upward.

The left leg kicks up in a big circle (*j*). Left leg still making a full and wide circle in *k*, and in *l* coming down to the lower bar. In *m*, the hand on the high bar comes down. A stride position on the low bar.

39*a*

9*e*

39*f*

39*g*

9*k*

39*l*

39*m*

# Flank from Stag Sit

One of the simplest dismounts and one that
is learned early.

**40.** A stag position that can be reached in
a number of ways such as skin the cat (*a*). In *b*
both legs are extended. Legs continue upward
to a V seat (*c*). Body weight is on the right
arm. Legs continue to extend down to the
landing (*d*, *e*, *f*, and *g*).

40*a*

40*d*

40*e*

40b

40c

40f

40g

# Flank Dismount from Front Support

This dismount can be done from either bar.

**41.** Front support (*a*). In *b* legs are swung forward forcefully. A good cast (*c*) with the hips high above the lower bar. Body weight is beginning to shift to the left hand. In *d*, legs are coming around.

Legs are clearing the bar (*e*). Right arm will be released. In *f*, nearing the floor. A stable landing with both arms overhead (*g*).

41*a*

41*b*

41*e*

41*f*

41c

41d

41g

Spotting: The left arm is supported. Spotter is
away from the side of leg clearance.

# Underswing Dismount

The dismount is shown off the low bar, though it can also be carried out from the high bar.

**42.** The movement starts from a front support (*a*), but there is no cast. Action is started by thrusting the shoulders back and a sharp pike with an effort to keep the hips close to the bar (*b*). In *c*, a kip position with the ankles to the low bar and the arms extended. The effort is to keep the legs going upward and forward. The hips rise. It's a lot like a kip. This kipping action continues in *d*. By *e* legs have shot upward and arms have pushed back.

Release of the bar (*f*) with feet moving toward the mat for the landing (*g*).

42a

42b

42e

42f

42c

42d

42g

## Underswing Dismount
## from the High Bar

**43.** We've looked at the underswing dismount off the low bar. As we said, the same dismount can be done from the high bar. The ideas are not at all different from the ones you have just seen on the low bar. You can see the same important features.

43*a*

43*d*

43*e*

43*b*

43*c*

43*f*

# Cast Straddle, Underswing Dismount

This should be taught first on the low bar. Later it can be done from the high bar, going in the other direction.

**44.** Start is from a front support (*a*). In *b*, legs thrust forward. By *c* legs have cast, and they straddle to move the feet on the bar.

Chest is compressed toward the legs in *d*. A pull of the arms and a push of the legs force the soles of the feet against the bar. In *e*, still compressed and the feet still against the bar.

Feet remain against the bar in *f*. Hips are coming out past the low bar, and continue to rise in *g*. They are being shot toward the ceiling in a kip action. The hips are still rising as the feet come together in *h*. Next, the high bar is released—actually thrown away or pushed

44*a*

44*b*

44*c*

44*g*

44*h*

44*i*

away (*i*). In *j*, clearing the low bar and coming to the ground.

The landing (*k*) and finish of the dismount (*l*).

Spotting: The spotter tries to make sure that the soles of the feet remain in contact with the high bar and that the hips are high enough to clear the low bar.

44e

44f

44k

44l

# Penny-Drop Dismount

**45.** Sitting on the low bar with the legs extended, arms grasping the high bar (*a*). Knees hook over the low bar and the hips are pushed up (*b*). In *c*, the hands are released. Body is extended and is starting to swing upward (*d*). The swing continues (*e*). The body reaches the height of the low bar. The legs begin to straighten.

The landing on the mat (*f*, *g*, and *h*).

45*a*

45*b*

45*e*

45*f*

45c

45d

45g

45h

## Half Seat Circle— Flank Cut Dismount

**46.** Seat on the high bar (*a*). Weight on the arms (*b*). Hips lifted off the bar. In *a*, pike position; falling backward.

Circling under of the hips ( *d*). In *e* hips rise as the circle continues.

Direction is reversed (*f*) and hips shoot toward the ceiling. In *g* legs shoot up close to the high bar. The left arm is ready to let go.

The release and a quarter turn (*h*). Body starts to extend, and full extension is reached in *l*.

Landing (*j*) and stand (*k*).

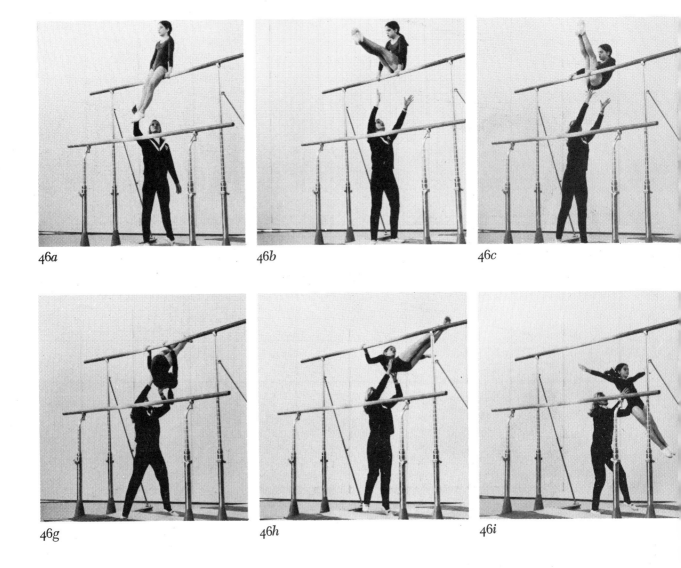

46*a*

46*b*

46*c*

46*g*

46*h*

46*i*

6d

46e

46f

6j

46k

# Handstand Dismount with Quarter Turn on Low Bar

A good dismount for advanced beginners or intermediates.

**47.** From a front support the hands have been released (*a*). A reach toward the low bar in *b*. Body is rotating forward. Ready for a mixed grip—a regular grip with the right hand, a reverse grip with the left hand (*c*). In *d*, extension, and on the way to a handstand, which appears in *e*.

The quarter turn is completed in *f* as the right hand is released. In *g* body is extended and in *h* approaching the floor, straight, and with arm up.

Landing (*i*) and arm is released (*j*)—the finish.

47*c*

47*g*

47*h*

47a

47b

47e

47f

47i

47j

# Hecht Dismount

**48.** Start of the cast from the front support (*a*). In *b*, using the momentum of the cast.

Extended position of the body as the lower bar is reached (*c*). In *d*, the lower bar forces the pike of the body. Wrap of the bar (*e*).

Now the "pop" off the lower bar is timed (*f*). Height! Arms rise and legs rise (*g*). An arch. In *h*, *i*, and *j*, the landing to the mat.

Spotting: In *e* the spotter tries to keep the "pop" off the lower bar from happening too soon. Help with height in *g*. In the landing the spotter keeps the gymnast from overrotation.

48a

48d

48g

48h

48b

48c

48e

48f

48i

48j

# COMBINATIONS

When we talk about combinations we mean the selection of two or more exercises that go well together. Combinations are meant to produce a smooth flow of action. One skill should provide momentum for the next move.

## Suggested Combination for Beginners (#1)

**49.** Hip pullover over the low bar (*a*, *b*, and *c*), one-leg shoot-through (*d*, *e*, and *f*), and front stride circle (*g* and *h*).

49*c*

49*d*

49*e*

49a

49b

9f

49g

49h

Movement to a rear seat with hands on high bar (*i*, *j*, and *k*). Skin the cat (*l–q*). Ends in sitting position with one foot on the lower bar.

A move to get both feet on the high bar (*r* and *s*), forward roll over the high bar with reverse grip (*t*, *u*, and *v*), and monkey turn (*w* and *x*).

49*i*

49*m*

49*n*

49*o*

49*s*

49*t*

49*u*

49*j*

49*k*

49*l*

49*p*

49*q*

49*r*

49*v*

49*w*

49*x*

Whip pike over low bar (*y–bb*), preparation
for the hip pull over the high bar (*cc*), and
hip pull over the high bar (*dd*, *ee*, and *ff*).

Kip to the lower bar (*gg*), legs extend (*hh*),
and penny-drop dismount (*ii–ll*).

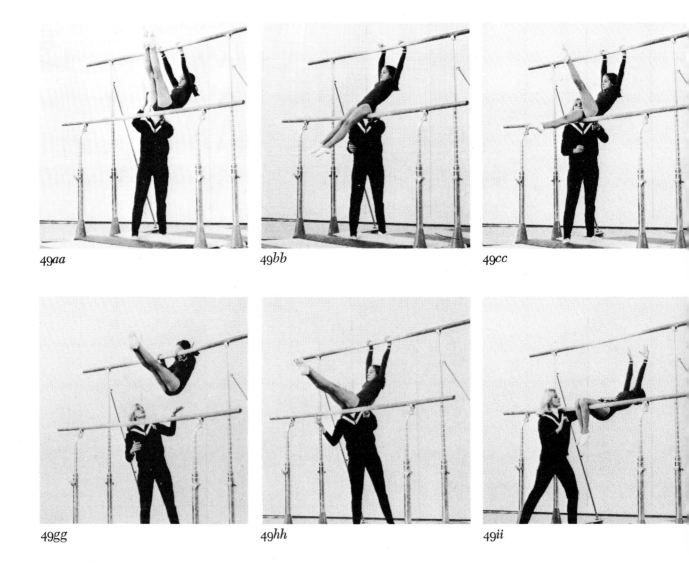

49*aa*

49*bb*

49*cc*

49*gg*

49*hh*

49*ii*

49y

49z

49dd

49ee

49ff

49jj

49kk

49ll

## Suggested Combination
## for Beginners (#2)

**50.** Flank vault mount (*a*, *b*, and *c*), underswing—half-turn wrap—from rear seat (*d–j*), and a single-leg shoot-through (*k*, *l*, and *m*).

50*a*

50*d*

50*e*

50*f*

50*j*

50*k*

50*l*

50b

50c

50g

50h

50i

50m

Front stride circle (front mill circle) (*n–s*)
to a sit position holding the high bar (*t* and *u*).

5o*n*

5o*o*

5o*p*

oq

5or

5os

5ot

5ou

# Suggested Combination
# for Beginners (#3)

This combination is taken from the middle of
a routine to a dismount.

**51.** Jump to a back hip circle on the high
bar (*a–e*), a cast back over the low bar (*f*, *g*,
and *h*), and "beat" of the low bar, with heels
kicking upward (*i* and *j*).

51*a*

51*b*

51*c*

51*f*

51*g*

51*h*

51d

51e

51i

51j

A straddle over the low bar ($k$ and $l$), a
long hip hang to the high bar ($m$–$r$), cast
straddle to high bar ($s$, $t$, and $u$), underswing
($v$ and $w$), half turn ($x$ and $y$).

51*n*

51*o*

51*p*

51*t*

51*u*

51*v*

1k  51l  51m

1q  51r  51s

1w  51x  51y

Wrap low bar (*z–dd*). Cast straddle underswing
dismount with half turn (*ee–ll*).

51*z*

51*dd*

51*ee*

51*ff*

51*jj*

51*kk*

51*ll*

51aa

51bb

51cc

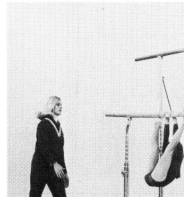

51gg

51hh

51ii

# Suggested Combination
# for Intermediates (#4)

**52.** Glide kip catch mount (*a–i*) and straddle over the low bar (*j, k,* and *l*).

52a                    52b                    52c

52g                    52h                    52i

*d*

52*e*

52*f*

*j*

52*k*

52*l*

Kip from low bar to high bar (*m–r*), and
cast wrap eagle (continues from previous kip
without an extra swing) (*s–z*).

52*m*

52*o*

52*p*

52*q*

52*u*

52*v*

52*w*

*…n*

*…r*

*52s*

*52t*

*…2x*

*52y*

*52z*

# ROUTINES

Your routine is a linking of skills that is meant to form a smooth and continuous performance all the way from the mount to the dismount. Your effectiveness will depend on making the best use of the skills you have mastered. And, of course, as you continue to learn, your routine will become more advanced.

In putting together a routine the beginner has a somewhat different problem than does the advanced gymnast. That's mostly because of the relatively few skills that are at the disposal of the beginner. The international gymnast can always meet the full difficulty requirements, whereas the beginner may have few or no medium-difficulty skills to include.

Even though the beginner may be far from able to carry out a routine used by an expert, it is useful for her to familiarize herself with the scoring rules that guide the expert. It is most helpful to see the road ahead.

Let's consider a few guidelines:

1. Try to keep the routine continuous and flowing. You won't be able to do this right away, but it is a good goal. Support positions should not be held. Instead, they are positions to go through. Again, you won't be able to do this at first, but it should be kept in mind. Try to avoid extra swings.

2. Variety, originality, and imagination are vital to setting up any effective routine.

3. Make use of both bars. The beginner can get as comfortable with the high bar as with the low bar.

4. Vary the direction in which you face. That is, don't always face the same bar.

5. Make the most of your skills. Don't feel rushed. Try for a good flow of action and big, or full, movements (amplitude).

6. Keep working on the glide kip. This movement takes time and patience, but it gets you ready to move from the beginning to the intermediate stage.

# Vaulting

## ABOUT VAULTING

Why should vaulting be so satisfying to do and so pleasing to watch? An over-all look at sports may supply an answer. As you know, for many thousands of years sports activities have had a place in the lives of people all over the world. Primitive people had their sports, and still do; but it does seem that sports flourish best in advanced civilizations. More than two thousand years ago the Greeks produced a culture so remarkable that we still cannot understand or explain it. The powerful effects of what was said and done in this relatively tiny community long ago are still strongly with us. This is certainly true in sports—think of the Olympic Games.

Over the centuries many sports have been devised. Those that have survived over a long period have a number of common ingredients. These are running, jumping, and propelling an object. The last of these ingredients, the object—such as a ball—is usually thrown, but it is also kicked, as in football or soccer.

Vaulting is popular because it has two of the ingredients that are valued in sports. There is a run, and there is a jump. There is the fascinating fun of flying through the air. And the excitement is increased when an object is cleared, such as a fence or a wall. Here the legs spring to supply the basic lifting force. But the arms can also be used both to increase lift and to direct the body. If you are clearing a wall or fence the use of your arms adds both to clearance and the fun of it all.

In vaulting you clear a "horse." Why is this piece of gymnastic apparatus called a horse? You can probably guess the answer. Mankind's past activities have often been associated with the horse. Perhaps the legacy of the modern gymnastic event comes most directly from the medieval knights. Their ability to perform and survive was dependent on their agility with reference to the horse. They had to be able to vault to it and then move about with confidence.

Even when the horse actually developed into a piece of gymnastic equipment, there was still a tendency to simulate its source, even to the extent of painting a head on one end and placing a tail on the other. In men's gymnastics another trace of the heritage is still there: the pommels represent parts of the saddle, and the exercises performed require great strength and agility, qualities needed and prized by the knights of old.

As you surely know by now, there has been a great and happy revolution in gymnastics. For a long time females simply imitated the events of males. Then they decided that something better could be done. The problem was how to stay within the great tradition of gymnastics and still make the events appropriate to girls. It worked out well. The uneven parallel bars is a good example of an excellent solution, and so is vaulting: it was decided to do away with pommels and to clear the horse from the side or at right angles to it.

But just to clear the horse never seemed enough. It became important to vault over the horse in the classical tradition of good form. So the graceful tumbling techniques that are so important to floor exercise and the balance beam are a vital part of vaulting. In looking at a good vault we always appreciate the flight path, but we are also impressed by the ways in which tumbling skills are carried out.

*The opportunity that vaulting offers.* When the gymnast competes in the four international events, the vault takes only a little bit of her competition time. The two vaults allowed actually consume only seconds. Perhaps this time factor creates a harmful illusion. The gymnast may unconsciously think that since the vault occupies a small part of competition, only a small part of practice time should be given to it. This may explain why the weak event of otherwise fine gymnasts tends to be the vault. A great opportunity is being missed. For one thing, the gymnast is deprived of the enormous satisfactions and sense of achievement that excellence in vaulting can bring. For another, vaulting makes up 25 per cent of the total score.

*How the vault is different.* The greatest difference between the vault and the other three gymnastic events is that the vault has no routine. In the other events a variety of skills are woven together to produce an over-all performance. In contrast, the vault is a single skill, sufficient by itself. A routine takes time. The vault is done within a matter of seconds. Though the vault requires the same grace as the other events, it is powerful, dynamic, and aggressive.

*Scoring.* As in the other events the highest possible score is ten, and a rating of ten is applied only to the advanced vaults. Deductions along the way determine the final score. The ceiling for scoring a vault is based on level of difficulty. The level assigned to a vault can change with review by the governing bodies.

# PARTS OF THE VAULT

Nearly all athletic events require a smooth and continuous flow of action. Motions blend into each other to produce a fine performance. Even so, it is useful to break down an event into various parts. In this way understanding and learning can be greatly increased. This process of analysis seems particularly useful in the case of the vault. But while we are looking at the parts of the vault, we must keep in mind that, to make a pleasing and effective performance, they must flow together.

For our purpose the best way of looking at the parts of the vault seems to be as follows.

*Approach*
*Take-off*
*Preflight*
*Action off the horse (or repulsion)*
*Afterflight*
*Landing*

Each of these divisions or parts will be talked about as we look at the various vaults. You will become more and more familiar with each part. Some parts are changed somewhat to meet the needs of a particular vault, but there are general points of form for each part that have carryover value. These common threads are what we will be considering in this section. And, later on, as we look at the different vaults, we'll be talking about the parts again.

*Approach.* The job is to build up speed by a run. How much speed? Well, early in your career you will be working on simple vaults that don't require great speed. But, as you get to more advanced vaults, speed becomes important. After all, speed is the power factor, supplying the energy that is at your disposal to carry out the vault. As you get further along, you will be more interested in speed of approach because it does determine how well the rest of the vault can be performed.

But speed has to be controlled speed. This is true in practically all athletics. You've got to feel that you are in control. The greatest sprinters in track events are always in complete control; with them it's never a scramble. You can compare your task to that of the pole vaulter, for his is very close to yours. The pole vaulter knows that the greater his speed down the runway, the more energy he will have for clearance of the bar. But he also knows that he has things to do as he takes off. He can't afford to be out of control. To summarize, then, you must work for the best combination of speed and control. Probably no athlete can run all-out with good control. But the great athletes keep working to approach full speed with control.

The other gymnastic events don't place a premium on running ability. For this reason the gymnast seldom pays enough attention to running form. But the girl who does develop good running form will surely have a big advantage in the vault. Her run will be faster and made with less effort. It will also become more reliable. She will be able to depend on it to get her to the right spot. Though the run is not an official part of the vault, the judges are human and are bound to be favorably influenced by its smoothness and grace.

Superb running form makes such an immediate over-all impression that we recognize its beauty at once. But if we look further we can see some of its features. First, there is relaxation. At any given moment the muscles that are not actually working are relaxed. This is particularly true during the recovery phase of the leg in striding. Arm action is smooth and regular. The body does not wobble back and forth. The feet are in alignment, which means that a line drawn from the heel to the toes would point in the direction of movement. Alignment of the feet is important for two reasons: it makes for more efficient running, and it helps prevent shin splints. Though not dangerous, shin splints are painful and interfere with practice.

In your early vaults you won't be able to make full use of the power provided by a full and efficient run. Yet it will pay to look ahead to when you will be carrying out advanced vaults. So, as you improve your vaulting ability, you improve your running.

At the end of your run you will want to strike a desired spot with one foot. It should be the same foot each time. Most right-handed athletes find that they get a better drive from the left foot. The opposite is usually true for left-handed athletes. The task is like that of the long jumper or pole vaulter in track and field. Each has to arrive at a spot with controlled speed. The first preparation is to work for good form and do lots of running. The main idea is to develop a stride that is consistent in length. The long jumper and pole vaulter use checkmarks as guides to beginning the approach. The distance of the checkmark from the take-off spot is measured with a tape. Of course, checkmarks are useful only when a lot of running has produced a consistent stride.

*Take-off.* A good reliable run and the correct use of the reuther board almost guarantee a fine upward take-off. The board itself is an ingenious kind of device combining a slope and a small amount of spring. The slope is the important factor, because it greatly aids the conversion of forward motion into upward motion. The run builds up energy, and the task is to use this energy to get height. If the jumpers in track and field were allowed to use such a slope, all world records would be quickly broken.

The last stride of the approach, the one that brings you to the board, is called the hurdle. The hurdle is not a jump. It is really a way of getting both feet to the board at the same time. There is no effort to lift. You think of remaining low and driving forward. Also, during the hurdle the body can be better positioned for the lift. The natural lean of running can be corrected. The body can be straightened to make the best use of the reuther board.

*Preflight.* You take off. You make contact with the horse. Between the take-off and contact with the horse there has to be a flight through the air, and this action is called the foreflight, or preflight. The preflight is an important part of the vault and strongly affects the scoring. The ideal, of course, is a long and well-controlled foreflight. But this can't happen right away. It comes only with increased speed, confidence, and skill. A long preflight requires a long distance between the board and the horse. The beginner should work with the board fairly close to the horse and then increase the distance between them as she progresses.

As you move along the way to more advanced vaults, preflight body position will change. Early vaults will use a bent-body ascent. Then you will go on to straight-body ascents. The highly advanced vaults will require a layout ascent.

In the final analysis the distance and height of the foreflight will depend on the speed at which you can hit the board and how well you can make use of the board. That's why you continue to work on the run as you develop other vaulting skills.

*Repulsion.* In all vaults your hands contact the horse after the preflight. The hands have two jobs to do. They serve as a pivot point about which the body rotates, and they push the body upward to increase height. This action is known as repulsion. The lifting function is especially vital. Lift of the body is needed for clearance of the horse and for a good afterflight.

In the more advanced vaults the arms have to be straight upon contact with the horse, and they must remain straight until the horse is left. Since the arms are not supposed to bend, the lifting power has to come from the hands and shoulders. Nevertheless, it's remarkable how much lift a skilled gymnast can obtain.

Speed of repulsion is an important characteristic of the good vaulter. Contact with the horse is only a matter of tiny fractions of a second. The advanced vaulter gives the impression that she treats the horse like a "hot stove." Even so, the drive off the horse is powerful.

*Afterflight.* The action from repulsion to landing is called the afterflight. The goal is a very long afterflight carried out with grace and good posture. Like a long preflight, a long afterflight comes after the gymnast's skill level becomes high. The long and graceful afterflight is the mark of an advanced gymnast. For the most part only the advanced vaults lend themselves to a full afterflight. As we have stressed, in nearly all athletic events the ability to carry out one act well depends on how well the preceding acts have been carried out. So it is with the afterflight. A good afterflight depends upon a good run, a good take-off, a good foreflight, and a good repulsion. When the previous acts are carried out well, the setting is there for a fine afterflight.

A good afterflight is in balance with the preflight in that they should both be about the same distance. Getting the two flights about equal should not be a great problem in normal learning, since they both depend upon speed and efficiency of execution.

*Landing.* Every vault should finish in a solid and balanced landing. Because the landing is the last part of the vault that judges see, it's bound to make a strong impression on them and influence the scoring.

The landings for the uneven parallel bars and the beam are similar to that for the vault. The same principles and techniques apply. Upon contact with the mat a slight bend of the knees helps to absorb the impact of landing. But the legs quickly straighten and a good solid position is taken. Even among good gymnasts there is sometimes a struggle for balance. Often they are forced to take an extra step because of imbalance, and this, of course, reduces the score.

The problem of getting a balanced landing in the vault is greater than that for the other events. That's because forward speed is greater. When there is forward motion of the body at landing, the upper body tends to rotate forward. If you were to land in a vertical position you would tend to pitch forward. To compensate for this tendency you must learn to land with the body tilted backward. The more speed, the greater the tilt.

# EQUIPMENT AND SAFETY

*The Horse.* This is the main piece of equipment. There's little point in describing the horse, because you can walk into almost any gymnasium and examine one. You will probably see pommels or grips on the horse. These are used only by men and are removed when the horse is used for girls' vaulting. You will notice that the horse is very heavy, with most of the weight in the base. That's because the horse has to be very stable. It's got to remain steady while taking the impact of a flying body.

Many gyms will have other equipment for vaulting. The Swedish box is popular and useful. Its great value is that it can be easily adjusted for a variety of vaulting heights.

*Mats.* These are, of course, needed to cushion the landing. As you look at the photos in this section you will see that the girls are using a mat of unusual thickness. This type of mat is known as a crash pad. The crash pad can absorb a great amount of shock. We hope your school has one; but if not, regular mats can do the job. They should, however, be placed in double thickness.

*Safety.* Most human activities, including sports, have a certain risk factor. But always the goal is to keep the chance of injury to a minimum. Safety depends largely on reliable equipment, sound progression, and good spotting. Sound progression simply means that you go on to an advanced skill only when you are ready for the advance. You and your coach will know when you're able to move along. A background that prepares you for the next step is perhaps the greatest of the safety factors. Spotting always remains important. A gymnast's interest in spotting is twofold. When you perform, you will want the best possible help from your spotter. But you too will take your turns as a spotter, and when that occurs, you will want to make your best contribution. You contribute best when you understand your event.

## Run and Take-Off

**1.** Running is an ongoing part of your program. You will become faster, smoother, and more confident. As your stride gets consistent, you will use checkmarks to help you finish the run at the right spot for the hurdle. The first vaults that you learn won't require much speed, but keep polishing your run with an eye toward the more advanced vaults when speed does become important.

*1a*

*1d*

*2a*

*2b*

1b

1c

**2.** It takes time and practice to make the best use of the reuther board in converting the energy of your run to body height. For much of your career you will be working to improve your take-off. A good initial orientation will make for better progress. An instructor or spotter can help you get the correct feel for the take-off and preflight.

2c

2d

# Dive Rolls—Bent-Body Ascent

Dive rolls are helpful in getting you ready for vaulting. You can get used to various parts of the vault. Since you don't have to be concerned about the horse, you are freer to get a feel for some of the basics. You can get used to a run, take-off, flight itself, and landing on the mat.

Your introduction to dive rolls will be with a bent-body ascent, because it's easier. Also, the early vaulting skills that you learn can be carried out with a bent-body ascent. When you first do dive rolls, you shouldn't worry about technique, because their chief purpose is orientation. Yet, as you progress, your dive rolls can include elements of good vaulting form.

Dive rolls should remain a part of your training routine. Even advanced vaulters use dive rolls for warm-ups. Later on, we'll be looking at dive rolls carried out with a straight-body ascent.

3a

**3.** Run has been made. A hurdle to the board (*a*). Flight starts (*b*). Body is relatively straight. In *c*, hips are high. Roll has started. In *d* hands make the first contact with the mat to cushion the fall.

From the hands to the shoulders (*e*). It's good to get in the habit of finishing in a standing position (*f* and *g*).

3d

3e

3b

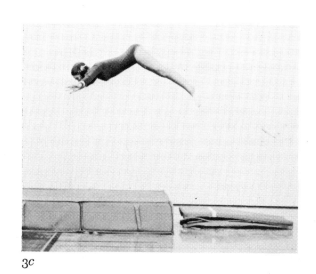

3c

3f

3g

# Squat Vault Demonstration

Introduction to the horse can come without a continuous vault. With the help of a good spotter you have a chance to get an orientation in stages. You can get used to the horse itself and the various phases of the vault.

The spotter lifts and steadies. In this way the vault is imitated with a kind of slow motion and pauses.

**4.** Positioning of the hands (*a*). Hips high on contact with the horse (*b*). Knees start moving through for the squat (*c*). In *d*, knees tucking toward chest, feet approaching horse. Position on the horse is held for orientation (*e*).

Jump from the horse (*f*) and the body straightens (*g*).

4*a*

4*d*

4*e*

4b

4c

4f

4g

## Straddle Vault

We've already looked at a photo sequence in which each step along the way was stopped for orientation. Here we go a bit further, and the only stop is made in a straddle position on top of the horse. Again, orientation and confidence are the goals of this training exercise. The pause on the horse gives the gymnast a good chance to concentrate on the landing.

Intensive spotting is not needed.

As you look at the photo sequence, it's important to remember that it is an orientation or training exercise. In carrying out this exercise you should not even try for the arm action in the take-off for the long foreflight that you will use later on as you progress.

**5.** Hurdle (*a*). Feet are low. In *b*, feet are together, legs slightly bent, upper body straight. In *c*, a slow and careful approach to the horse.

Take-off (*d*). Hands in contact with the horse. Hips rise. In *e* hip height lets the feet rise higher than the horse. Spotter steadies the arms. In *f*, landing on the horse (later on, in the straddle vault, the feet will clear the horse).

Ready to leave the horse (*g*) and airborne for the descent (*h*). In *i*, the landing. An erect position on the mat (*j*).

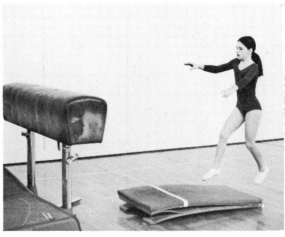

5*a*

5*d*

5*g*

5*h*

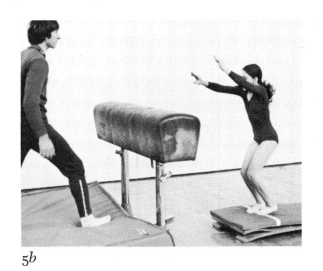

5b

5c

5e

5f

5i

5j

# Dive Roll over the Horse—Bent-Body Ascent

You can see that this exercise fits nicely into your progression. Up until now your workouts have been aimed toward a number of goals. You have been improving your approach so that you can run with greater speed and confidence. Your dive rolls have been getting you used to being airborne and landing. You have been carrying out exercises that give you a feel for the horse.

Now it's time to go back to the dive rolls. But this time, the horse is present. The need to clear the horse helps to emphasize a good run and a solid take-off. The improved run and take-off produce height. You find that you can clear the horse with ease and lots of room to spare. This improves your confidence and gets you ready for actual vaulting.

Since in the next steps in your progression your first vaults will be carried out with a bent-body ascent, the dive rolls over the horse will also employ a bent-body ascent.

**6.** Beginning of the hurdle (*a*). Body is kept low. In *b*, good height over the horse. Hips are lifting. Hands are ready to make contact for the landing in *c*. On landing, the roll has continued (*d*).

Movement to a standing position of attention just to get the habit (*e* and *f*).

6a

6d

6b

6c

6e

6f

## Squat Vault

With the squat vault we will be entering the realm of actual vaulting. By starting with the squat vault we will be following in the path of nearly every famous gymnast. It was their first vault, too.

The squat vault has no international rating and is never used in advanced competition. Yet even fine gymnasts continue to use it for both warm-up and review of basic principles of vaulting. Mastery of the squat vault leads to mastery of more advanced vaults. As you move along in your career, you won't use the squat vault in competition. But you can use it in your early meets and then keep it as a warm-up exercise.

When we dealt with the orientation exercises, the board was very close to the horse. Now the board is farther back to allow for the preflight.

7a

**7.** Hurdle almost completed (*a*). Body low. Feet are together for a landing on the reuther board. In *b*, take-off. Contact with the horse (*c*). Arms are straight and at a good angle to be ready for repulsion and an afterflight. By *d* the push from the horse (repulsion) has been made. Feet have plenty of room to clear the horse.

The body starts to straighten (*e*). In *f*, contact has been made with the mat. The body is slightly tilted back. Finish is in a balanced position (*g*).

7d

7e

7b

7c

7f

7g

## Straddle Vault

You've already used a form of the straddle
vault as an exercise. As you now know, the
straddle vault lends itself well to a stop position
on the horse. Hence, it can be used to provide
orientation. The next step in progress is to
clear the horse without the stop.

**8.** Approach (*a*) and take-off (*b*). In *c*,
contact with the horse. Hips are rising. Straddle
starts.

Clearance has been made (*d*). The push of
the fingers has helped attain body height.
In *e*, upper body moves upward and backward.
Legs close. Readiness for the landing.

An erect position (*f*).

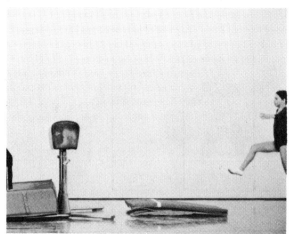

*8a*

*8d*

*8b*

*8c*

*8e*

*8f*

# Flank Vault

This vault is called "flank vault" because you clear the horse on your side. It's a highly useful vault in your progression. Good orientation to body position is afforded. Also, you carry out the interesting feat of removing one hand from the horse and depending on the other for the push-off.

The flank vault can be done from either side. Most vaulters have a natural or favorite side. From the standpoint of orientation, however, it's a good idea to master the flank from either side. In learning the flank vault you've got to cooperate with your spotter. The spotter has to know which side you will use.

**9.** Hurdle has been made—ready for the take-off (*a*). In *b*, foreflight with slight pike. Hands are moving toward the horse. Hands have reached the middle of the horse in *c*. Hips are rising. Flank movement has started with the legs straight and together. Body weight is shifting over the left hand. In *d* hips are high. Legs have good clearance of the horse. They remain straight and together. The left arm is doing the work off the horse as the right arm leaves to make room for the legs to come through.

Body height shows that there has been a good repulsion (*e*). Legs are back in alignment (*f*). In *g*, body is tilted slightly back on landing. Erect finishing position (*h* and *i*).

9*a*

9*d*

9*g*

9b

9c

9e

9f

9h

9i

## Thief Vault

For a number of reasons the thief vault is introduced early in your career. It has great value both in building confidence and affording orientation. Especially, this vault helps get you used to flying through the air. The thief is a fun vault to do and sustains interest and excitement. When you first start competing in meets for beginners, you can use the thief as a rather spectacular vault, a vault that pleases the audience.

Up until now you have been able to view the landing spot as you leave the horse. The thief vault introduces you to a kind of "blind" landing. During repulsion and the first part of the afterflight you can't see the spot where your feet are going to touch down. Getting used to this kind of landing is important as you go on to more advanced vaults.

Curiously, the thief is the only vault where the take-off is made from one foot.

**10.** A long stride to the board (*a*). Take-off from one foot (*b*). Lead leg starts to rise (*c*). In *d* lead leg is higher than the horse. Take-off has been completed.

Take-off leg is nearing the lead leg (*e*). Hands are still not in contact with the horse. Legs high and straight (*f*) as repulsion starts. Finish of repulsion (*g*). Hips are forward. Legs remain straight.

A good afterflight (*h*) and landing (*i*).

10*a*

10*d*

10*g*

10b

10c

10e

10f

10h

10i

# Stoop Vault

The stoop vault shows a logical progression from the previous vaults. In the squat vault you raised your feet by bending your legs. In the straddle you spread your legs for more foot height. And in the flank vault your legs were raised to one side. But in the stoop vault the legs remain straight and pass under the body.

You can quickly see that if the legs are to remain straight and be under the body the hips have to be high. This means a faster run, a stronger take-off, and a stronger repulsion. In short, your previous work prepares you for the stoop vault.

**11.** Run and hurdle have been completed and take-off is underway in *a*. A good foreflight (*b*). Hips are moving upward. Hands are ready to make contact with the horse. In *c*, a forceful repulsion. The fine hip height will allow the feet to clear the horse with ease. By *d*, legs have swung forward between the arms. They remain straight and together. Upper body is rising.

Landing (*e*). Body is tilted slightly backward so that the landing can be more stable.

11*a*

11*d*

11b

11c

11e

## Pike Headspring Vault

The headspring vault is surely a milestone in your progress. For the first time you carry out a vault that uses a full rotation of the body. The skills that you have been learning prepare you for the headspring.

The feeling of carrying out a headspring probably won't be entirely new to you, because it's likely that you've done them in your training for floor exercise. If not, however, practice the headspring on the mat before trying it on the horse.

We will be looking at three photo sequences. The first sequence (Fig. 12) shows a demonstration or training procedure. The action is slow, with stops along the way. The idea is to get an orientation or feeling for the positions of the vault. The spotter's help is important. In fact, the spotter lifts and holds the gymnast through the vault.

The actual vaults (Figs. 13 and 14) give us a chance to examine the essential parts of the pike headspring.

**12.** The gymnast simply walks (*a*). There is no run and no hurdle. Spotter is ready on the landing side of the horse. In *b* hands are reaching to the horse. There is no foreflight. A jump toward pike position (*c*). Spotter supports the wrist and makes sure that the head is lowered. Pike headstand position is held (*d*).

Hips now move slightly forward (*e*). Legs start to move upward and outward and arms begin to straighten (*f*). With the hips ahead and the body straight a push-off is made (*g*).

The body remains straight (*h*) and ready for the landing (*i*).

12*a*

12*d*

12*g*

12*b*

12*c*

12*e*

12*f*

12*h*

12*i*

**13.**  Hurdle is completed in *a* and gymnast is in take-off position. In *b*, the take-off. Hands reach the horse in *c*. Head is ready to tuck under. This is a pike position with the hips high.

Hips move forward (*d*). Body starts to straighten and by *e* is arched. Good repulsion. Spotter is ready to support for height if needed. In *f*, body is straight. Legs are together and straight. Upper body is rising as the legs lower.

Ready for landing with the body tilted back (*g*). Erect position (*h*).

13*a*

13*b*

13*e*

13*f*

13c

13d

13g

13h

**14.** Take-off has been made in *a* and hips are rising. Hands are on the horse. In *b*, pike position. Hips are high. Head is being partially tucked. Spotter is ready to make sure that hands stay in good contact with the horse. In *c* pike is now full. Body continues to rotate. Top of the head makes contact with the horse. By *d* hips have moved forward past the shoulders. Almost ready for the repulsion. Legs are beginning to snap forward and up. Repulsion has been made in *e*. Body is straight. Spotter ready to help if need be.

An erect and balanced landing (*f*).

14a

14b

14c

14d

14e

14f

## Pike Handspring

After you have worked on the pike headspring, a natural step is to go on to the pike handspring. You will be using a faster run, a more efficient hurdle, and a more explosive take-off. You will recall that in the headspring you spent considerable time on the horse. In the handspring there will be less time and less action on the horse. There will be a stronger repulsion with the arms straight and the shoulder girdle doing the work.

**15.** A low and fast hurdle (*a*). The feet are coming together. In *b* take-off has been made. A bent-body ascent with hands moving toward the horse. Arms are straight.

Pike position on the horse (*c*). Spotter steadies the gymnast's wrist on the horse and is ready to help with body height. Body is straightening in *d* and repulsion is underway. By *e* push-off has been made. Body has a slight arch. Contact with the mat is made (*f*). Body is tilted back to make for a stable landing.

Landing and an erect position (*g* and *h*).

15*a*

15*b*

15*e*

15*f*

15c

15d

15g

15h

# Dive Roll—
# Straight-Body Ascent

The advanced vaults require a straight-body
ascent from the reuther board. So the next step
along the road to greater progress is the
mastery of this ascent.

Very early in your training you started to
carry out dive rolls with a bent-body ascent.
This important orientation procedure helped
you to learn a series of vaults. We hope you have
been continuing your dive rolls as a part
of your warm-ups.

Because a straight-body ascent is needed
for the more advanced vaults, your dive rolls
more and more begin to emphasize the straight
body during the flight. As before, the great
value of the dive roll lies in the freedom it
affords. You are free to concentrate on the
basics without being concerned with a full vault.

**16.**   Hurdle (*a*). By *b* take-off has been
made. Body remains straight during ascent and
is still straight in *c*.

Hands contact the mat (*d*). Body now bends
to allow a smooth landing. In *e*, a roll over the
shoulders to the back. Roll continues (*f*).
Standing position (*g*).

16*a*

16*d*

16*e*

16b

16c

16f

16g

# .Dive Roll over Horse—
# Straight-Body Ascent

At first, the dive roll is carried out without
the horse. But the value of the training exercise
is increased even more when it is carried out
over the horse. Strong lift off the board is
emphasized. Also, the gymnast gets used to
carrying out a straight-body ascent with the
horse present.

**17.** In *a*, a fine lift. Straight body during the
ascent. Straight-body position is held in *b*
as horse is cleared. In *c*, start of the roll to the
shoulders and back. Roll continues (*d*) to
standing position (*e*).

17*a*

17*d*

17b

17c

17e

## Horizontal Squat

You are now beginning to work on the straight-body-ascent vaults. In this series the horizontal squat is usually the first to be learned. As with other advanced vaults, the run is faster, the take-off more explosive, and the repulsion stronger.

**18.** A strong take-off has been made (*a*). Body is straight during ascent and preflight (*b*). Legs are rising (*c*) and will be above the horizontal on contact with the horse. In *d*, spotter ready to steady wrist of gymnast. Start of the squat.

18*a*

18*b*

18*e*

18*f*

A strong repulsion has lifted the upper body. Knees are tucked close to the chest. In *f*, the descent, with spotter ready to control amount of body rotation. Landing (*g* and *h*).

18*c*

18*d*

18*g*

18*h*

# Horizontal Straddle

You've already had some experience in straddling the horse. The straddle vault that you have worked with was carried out with a bent-body ascent. When performed with a straight-body ascent the straddle vault becomes more spectacular. Also, it is considered an advanced vault and yields more points for difficulty.

It's important to realize that as you move on to the more advanced vaults a greater premium is placed on a fast run, a strong take-off, and a powerful repulsion.

**19.** Take-off (*a*). The run has been faster and the take-off stronger than in early vaults. Contact with the horse being made in *b*. Body is now horizontal, with the hips still rising. Legs start to straddle in *c* and the body to pike. Head up. Knees straight. By *d*, the horse has been cleared. Legs are coming together. Shoulders are moving upward and backward.

Landing (*e*) and erect position (*f*).

19*a*

19*d*

19b

19c

19e

19f

# Horizontal Stoop Vault

You already know that the stoop vault is a
progression from the squat and straddle vaults.
That's because the legs are swung like a
pendulum. The legs are straight and under the
body. So in order to clear the horse there has
to be more power all along the way, including
run, take-off, and repulsion.

20a

**20.** Straight-body ascent has been made
(*a*). Body is horizontal as the horse is
approached. Pike brings the hips high. Repulsion
brings the body even higher (*b*). There is
lots of room for the legs to clear the horse.
By *c*, repulsion has contributed to good height.
Legs have come through between the arms.

Straightening of the body and landing (*d*)
and erect position (*e*).

20d

**21.** There has been a straight-body ascent.
Gymnast is moving toward the horizontal
position (*a*). In *b*, contact with the horse.
Hips are rising. Repulsion has started.

Clearance of the horse in the stoop
position (*c*).

21a

20b

20c

20e

21b

21c

## Layout Squat Vault

The layout vaults represent the next stage in progress. The layout supplies the base for truly advanced vaults. We've been working on straight-body ascents. The layout is a straight-body ascent, but it goes a step further in difficulty and spectacular appeal.

Thus far in the straight-body ascents you have been reaching the horse in a horizontal position or with your body about parallel to the floor. In the layout the body is higher than the horizontal. It is general practice for the judges to credit you with a layout only when the body is at an angle of 30 degrees or more above the horizontal upon contact with the horse.

You can see that the layout is bound to involve a long foreflight and greater height. This means a faster run and a more powerful take-off.

22a

**22.** A fast run and hurdle has placed the gymnast in good take-off position in *a*. Body is well back. In *b*, a strong lift from the board. Contact with the horse (*c*). Body is high— at least the required 30 degrees.

A powerful repulsion has been made by *d*. Hips have been driven high in the air, allowing lots of clearance past the horse. Body straightens (*e*) during descent.

A slight tilt backward upon landing (*f*) and erect position (*g*).

22d

22e

22b

22c

22f

22g

# Layout Straddle Vault

In carrying out the layout straddle your basic approach is similar to that used in the layout squat. You work for a fast and reliable run, a powerful take-off, full preflight—and, of course, the layout position with the body higher than the horizontal upon contact with the horse.

**23.** Readiness for a strong take-off (*a*). Contact with the horse (*b*). Body is about 30 degrees above the horizontal. A powerful repulsion has been made by *c*. Good height of the hips. Legs are straddled.

Body is straightening in *d*. Legs are coming together. Landing (*e*) and erect position (*f*).

23*a*

23*d*

23b

23c

23e

23f

**24.** Take-off (*a*) and long preflight (*b*). Body is straight and rising. It will be above 30 degrees when the horse is reached. Body has risen toward the vertical in *c*. Arms remain straight. Legs begin the straddle. Spotter is ready to support wrists.

By *d* a strong repulsion has added to body height. Good clearance. Legs are kept straight during the straddle.

Landing (*e* and *f*).

24*a*

24*b*

24c

24d

24e

24f

# Handspring Vault—Layout

The handspring marks another important milestone in your gymnastics career. Under the present rules the handspring is regarded as an advanced vault and is seen in top-level competition. And it provides a gateway for the mastery of other advanced vaults.

All of the basics and skills that you have been learning become more and more important. They afford the readiness to learn the handspring. Especially needed are a faster and surer run, an efficient hurdle, an explosive take-off, and a powerful and quick repulsion.

So important is the handspring that it is well worth while to look at several photo sequences. In the first series of pictures we will be looking at very heavy spotting. This training series is aimed at orientation. With the help of the spotters the gymnast is guided through the various positions and in this way gets a feel for the critical parts of the handspring vault.

**25.** Preflight (*a*). Two spotters are present, but they will be less active than in the previous sequence. In *b*, contact with the horse. Hands are in the center of the horse at shoulder width. Body is at an angle of about 45 degrees. In *c*, a strong repulsion starts. Good afterflight appears in *d*. Body arches.

Landing (*e*).

25a

25d

25b

25c

25e

**26.** A good lift results from a fast run and explosive take-off (*a*). Contact with effective body angle (*b*). Repulsion (*c*) adds to body height.

Descent at an angle (*d*) and solid landing (*e*).

26a

*26b*

*26c*

*26d*

*26e*

**27.** Hurdle underway (*a*). First spotter ready. In *b* take-off is being made. By *c* body is straight and lifting. Spotter guides.

Body remains straight as it reaches the horizontal (*d*). Rotation of the body continues in *e*. Contact with the horse will be made with the body at an angle of about 45 degrees. Second spotter is on far side of horse. By *f*, repulsion is just being completed. Spotter has one hand on the gymnast's arm and the other on the lower back.

Body is arched (*g*) and in *h* straightens. Spotter helps guide the descent. Landing is with legs bent slightly to cushion the contact (*i*). In *j*, to an erect position.

27a

27d

27g

27h

27b

27c

27e

27f

27i

27j

## Handspring Vault
## —a Further Look

**28.** and **29.** As you look at these additional photo sequences, you will again see some of the important features of the handspring vault. You will note a high and powerful take-off, straight body position during the preflight, body angle upon contact with the horse, strong repulsion, and a solid landing.

28a

28d

28e

29c

28b

28c

29a

29b

29d

29e

# Yamashita Vault

The Yamashita is one of the more recent of the advanced vaults. It was introduced at the Olympic Games by a Japanese gymnast. Because this vault was so spectacular and so appealing to both judges and audiences, it began to be used by top gymnasts all over the world. For a time it looked as though the Yamashita was appropriate only for world class performers. If this book had been written a few years ago, the Yamashita would not have been included. But we now know that a well-motivated and well-trained girl can indeed master this vault.

The Yamashita can be viewed as an extension of the handspring—as a type of handspring vault requiring more power and better timing. Mastery of the handspring certainly is in itself a great triumph, but the ambitious gymnast will want to go on to the Yamashita.

**30.** Speed and power are expressed in the long foreflight (*a*). Upon contact with the horse (*b*) body angle is great—here the angle is greater than 50 degrees. By *c*, action has taken place quickly and powerfully. Repulsion has been fast and strong. Body is high in the air in a pike position. In *d*, descent as the body straightens (*d*).

Photo *e* is highly significant. Look at the great distance from the horse to the landing spot. The long foreflight has been matched by an equally long afterflight. A long foreflight and a long afterflight are prized, but when they are equal in distance, the entire performance is enhanced. The angle of the legs helps put the brakes on the enormous velocity that has been generated.

Erect and solid landing (*f*).

30*a*

30*d*

30b

30c

30e

30f

## Yamashita Vault
## —a Further Look

**31.** and **32.** A further look at the
Yamashita. You can see how vital and dynamic
this vault is. It expresses athletic proficiency
and the results of sound training.

31a

31b

32a

32b

31c

31d

32c

32d

# *A Last Word*

---

It is hoped that this book has influenced you and that you will enter the most rewarding and delightful area of gymnastics. Along the way some wonderful young ladies have been your guides. They may be a little like you. They are not yet ready for Olympic competition but they do enjoy the exciting world of gymnastics.

When you give your time and energies to gymnastics, you can be assured of the satisfaction of achievement—and sometimes there is the thrill of winning. But gymnastics gives back so much that every girl is a winner.